Valiant Heart Trilogy

Book 1: Airship of Dreams
Book 2: The Call to Arms
Book 3: Blood and Fire

BLOOD AND FIRE

C.M.S. Thornton

Copyright © C.M.S. Thornton 2024

The right of C.M.S. Thornton to be identified as author of this work has been asserted by her in accordance with the Copyright, Designs and Patents Act, 1988.

All rights reserved. No part of this book may be reproduced or transmitted by any person or entity (including Google, Amazon or similar organisations) in any form or by any means, electronic or mechanical, including photocopying, recording or by any information storage and retrieval system, without prior permission in writing from the publisher.

A catalogue record for this book is available from the National Library of Australia.

Author: Thornton, C.M.S., author.
Title: Blood and fire : the hero who conquered the skies / C.M.S. Thornton.
ISBN: 9781923212046 (hardcover)
ISBN: 9781923212053 (paperback)

Series: Thornton, C.M.S. Valiant heart ; 3.
Notes: Includes bibliographical references.
Subjects: Biography--Non fiction.
Genre: Non fiction.

www.leavesofgoldpress.com
ABN 67 099 575 078

BLOOD AND FIRE

The Hero Who Conquered the Skies

Squadron Leader William Palstra M.C., B.A.

1891 - 1930

First World War soldier and airman

~ Salvation Army ~

~ 39th Battalion, Australian Imperial Force ~

~ Australian Flying Corps ~

~ University of Melbourne ~

~ Royal Australian Air Force ~

'Nobody would have guessed—least of all himself—
that beneath the waistcoat of this humble office clerk
there beat the heart of a leader of men
and a conqueror of the skies . . .'

*This book is dedicated to the families of the Australians and New Zealanders
who took part in the Great War 1914-1918;
also to the Palstras, the Holdaways,
and my sisters.*

W & K　　R101 THE WORLD'S LARGEST AIRSHIP　No 199.

CONTENTS

Introduction 1

Prologue 3

Palstra Family Tree. 12

Recap of Book 2 The Call to Arms 15

Part I: 1917

    1. The Western Front 19

    2. In the Trenches 31

    3. Magnum Opus 47

    4. Mud and Blood 67

    5. Victory and Glory. 83

    6. The Menin Gate and Broodseinde Ridge 103

    7. Passchendaele 111

Part II: 1917-1918

    1. Wings and Kings 115

    2. Flying Machines 121

    3. The Military Cross 125

    4. 1918: Flying School 129

    5. A Fully Fledged Pilot 141

    6. Back on the Front Line 153

    7. Attack on the Hindenburg Line 163

    8. The Americans Advance 171

    9. The Breaking of the Hindenburg Line 177

    10. The Beginning of the End 183

    11. Leave in Paris 203

PART III: 1919

    1. Repatriation 217

    2. Homecoming 223

    3. In memory of The Australian Imperial Force (AIF) 231

INTRODUCTION

The house of my childhood was haunted.

History permeated our family life, for it had soaked into the very fabric of the walls. It seeped from the antiques and curios brought back by our globe-trotting ancestors—the Chinese and Dutch ornaments, and the Māori artefacts. The past lurked, too, in the photograph albums, the wooden aeroplane propeller in the hall cupboard, the shoe-boxes filled with slightly tarnished AIF 'rising sun' buttons and badges, the handful of shrapnel, the old upright piano, the derelict chicken coop at the bottom of the garden, the old wooden sea-trunk in my bedroom, plastered all over with faded P&O steamship luggage labels that hinted at long-ago journeys to exotic places...

Ghosts, nameless and silent, were central to that history, emanating from memories that were not our own. Throughout the years, as my sisters and I grew up, these wraiths walked among us, pervading the waking hours and dreams of the adults. With every solemn tick of the vintage clock on the mantelpiece, they gradually increased their power over us, too.

The adults were unable to escape the influence of the past, let alone shield the children. There was nothing deliberate on their part; they did not intend to transmit the hauntings that bled into our young bones, but it happened. They were not conscious of it, and nor were we. There was no name for this phenomenon then, but there is now: 'Inter-generational trauma'.

We children did not yet understand it, but one 'present absence' in particular was the focus of unspeakable, long-buried anguish and longing. His legacy continues to affect our family to this day, almost a hundred years after his death.

A massive bureau, or chest-of-drawers, stood in the hallway of my childhood home. Made of age-darkened mahogany, it contained a hidden compartment; a long, low, deep drawer with no handles, which appeared, to the uninitiated, to be part of the decoration. Only those who were aware of its existence knew the trick of opening it. Within that drawer, known only to members of the immediate family, a multitude of old letters and diaries lay concealed for decades.

These faithfully preserved letters and diaries were written by, and to, my mother's father. For it was he whose terrible absence was the vortex into which the threads of our young lives were being drawn, and the burden we were destined to bear.

For as long as I can remember, an irresistible need to do the impossible, to bring him back to life, has ridden on the shoulders of me and my loved ones, like some demon. We each coped in our own way.

When I reached adulthood, my way of coping was to use the letters and diaries concealed in that hidden drawer to tell his story. I was also able to include many of the intriguing sepia photos from the well-preserved family albums.

Inter-generational trauma drove me to document his life almost day-by-day, extrapolating to fill the gaps in the first-hand material. This gave me around 632,000 words. Having condensed them (which was incredibly difficult), I have finally completed the duty that seemed to be laid upon me at birth. In the only way possible have (I hope), after decades of work and longing, immortalised my grandfather, William Palstra.

C.M.S. Thornton

PROLOGUE

Every event has consequences. Those consequences can ripple far across the universe, far into the future. In truth, they never really fade, even when we are no longer aware of them. After the primal event has passed out of human knowledge, still the effects flow inexorably on.

When His Majesty's airship R.101 fell out of the sky in 1930, her terrible ending seemed to herald the fading of the most far-reaching empire the world has ever known. It caused other effects, too—powerful enough to impact the lives of generations. Effects that, to this day, continue to reverberate through time and space . . .

On the evening of October 4th, 1930, rain-clouds were piling up in the skies over Bedfordshire, England.

At the Cardington Air Base, the British Empire's new airship, the largest object ever to fly, hovered two hundred feet above the ground, looking like some surreal deep-sea fish. She was tethered by the nose to the top of her mooring mast. A dazzling beam from a flood-lamp pierced the gathering dusk. Against the darkening skies, the massive hull of the cigar-shaped dirigible shimmered silver-grey. She floated parallel to the fields below, where a large crowd milled about, their faces upturned, marvelling at the sight. Surely this this improbable machine was too huge, too cumbersome to be suspended magically in the air, trembling slightly in the breeze, like a leaf!

The R101 being hauled to her mooring mast

With a length of 237 m (777 ft) the R.101 airship was longer than three Boeing 747s. That is more than twice the length of an international soccer pitch, or 2 ½ times the length of an American football field.

Though built to float, she weighed approximately one hundred and eighty tons; far more when fully loaded. Her motors, carried in five egg-shaped gondolas supported beneath the hull, were compression ignition engines developing five hundred and eighty-five horsepower each, and burning heavy oil. The R.101 was indeed a spectacular sight; a leviathan looming against the rain-clouds like some flying monster from an alien world.

Thousands of spectators lined the roads bordering the Air Base, whose gates were closed to the general public. Rows of parked motor-cars, head-lamps blazing, helped to illuminate the scene.

THE R101 AT CARDINGTON MOORING MAST

At 7.36 p.m. the great airship cast off from her mooring mast and began to rise.

'Hurrah! Hurrah!' chorused the spectators. 'God speed! Good luck!'

To the roar of enthusiastic cheering from the cap-waving crowd below, she slowly gained height, buoyed by the five million cubic feet of hydrogen gas sealed within her envelope. The crew of the airship evidently heard the cheering, and responded by flashing their lamps.

This was the beginning of the R.101's first international voyage, and she was bound for India. Her first stop was to be Ismailia, on the Suez Canal in Egypt, for re-fuelling. The 54 men on board—48 crew members and six passengers—were preparing to enjoy a long, comfortable flight.

On completion, the R.101 boasted luxurious passenger accommodation and service to rival that of the greatest ocean liners. Her sumptuous outfitting could be compared to the ship *RMS Titanic*. Potted palms and Axminster carpet adorned the elegant dining room. The dinner service had been specially commissioned, and bore her insignia. The airship officers wore dark blue uniforms. Their caps bore the blue and gold badge embroidered with 'Airship R.101', topped by a crown representing King George V.

Dining room of the R101 with the chief steward, Albert Savidge.

Passengers in the lounge room of the R101

The R.101 was to be among the first of a fleet of commercial dirigibles, 'liners of the skies', capable of carrying huge numbers of passengers back and forth across the globe.

The huge volumes of hydrogen gas carried in bags inside the airship's envelope made her lighter than air. It also made her highly flammable. Passengers and crew had to wear shoes without nails in the soles, lest the steel strike sparks. Smoking was forbidden, except in the specially fire-proofed 'smoking room'.

The R.101 had been carefully trimmed before leaving the mast. As she slipped her mooring cable she gave a slight lurch—watchers recalled that she dipped sharply—so Captain Irwin ordered four tons of water ballast to be dropped at once from the bows and amidships, in order to gain height. A warning from the meteorological office had told him to expect winds of up to forty to fifty miles per hour, worse than any conditions a British airship had experienced over land in the past.

The airship swung easily clear on an almost level keel, and very slowly wheeled away to gain height. Moving steadily south, she sent out regular radio messages so that her course could be followed. She circled around the nearby town of Bedford before rising to a thousand feet, then to fifteen hundred feet as she moved towards London.

Soon after she left Cardington, rain began to fall.

The R101 in flight

As the R.101 passed across England heading for the coast, householders peered out of their upper storey windows, eager to see the famous dirigible they had read about in the newspapers. They could see her huge bulk passing by, above the tree-tops. Her lights illuminated the surrounding landscape, glinting on silver spears of rain that stabbed through the darkness. Had the householders been able to look through the airship's windows into the interior, they might have glimpsed the passengers and officers gathered on the promenade deck, enjoying the view of the ground below.

The experienced crew on board expressed no concerns about the airship's performance in their wireless messages. At 9.21 p.m. the airship reported, 'Over London, All well. Moderate rain . . . course now set for Paris.' The message also gave the wind speed as 25 miles an hour—less than anticipated.

Being so heavily laden with passengers, luggage, fuel and water ballast, the airship continued to gain altitude slowly. She was still flying quite low when she passed over London, and her own radioed description of her manoeuvre before crossing the hills to the south was, 'Gradually increasing height so as to avoid high land'.

Near Hastings she left the English coast.

So vast was her envelope that a film of water only one sixty-fourth of an inch thick (0.4 mm) on the fabric would add eight tons to her weight. It was raining hard over the English Channel and, burdened beneath the weight of the downpour, the great silver dirigible fought her way with some difficulty, a thirty-five mile an hour sou-wester hammering on her starboard beam.

As she passed over the sea, a moderately serious engine problem occurred. The winds picked up and she slowly lost height until she reached the alarmingly low altitude of about seven hundred and fifty feet. Those on board could see the white caps of the foaming waves below.

At 10 p.m., the height coxswain, whose sole responsibility was maintaining correct altitude, received a visit from the first officer, Lieutenant Commander Atherstone. The more experienced airship pilot took over the wheel himself for a while until he had managed to achieve a considerable increase in altitude. Then he handed back the controls to the coxswain, warning him not to let the R.101 go below a thousand feet again.

By the time the R.101 had reached the French coast the engineers had corrected the mechanical problem. She made France over the Point de St Quentin and set a course direct for Paris. Strong winds were pummelling her vast envelope, and rain poured down in torrents.

At midnight, the airship sent out a further message. In spite of the rough weather conditions and serious trouble in maintaining height, its words betrayed no real fears on the part of the airship's guests and crew—

> After an excellent supper our distinguished passengers smoked a final cigar and having sighted the French coast have now gone to bed to rest after the excitement of their leavetaking.
>
> All essential services are functioning satisfactorily. The crew have settled down to watch-keeping routine.

R.101 sent out a regular position report at 1.28 am. At 1.30 she passed over the village of Saint-Valery-sur-Somme, appearing so low that the inhabitants scrambled from their beds, certain she would scrape the rooves off their houses. Slowly the airship thundered away into the pitch-dark night.

She sent another routine wireless transmission at 1.51, by which time she was approaching Beauvais, north of Paris. As she passed slightly to the east of the town, the roar of her engines awoke the townsfolk and frightened the children. People rushed to the windows to catch a glimpse of this historic sight; the majestic dirigible flying over their heads with her red and green warning lights twinkling, buffeted by rain and storm clouds.

After 2.07 a.m. there were no more messages from the R.101. Just outside Beauvais, with no warning at all, she went into a steep dive. She tilted so sharply that the engineers manning the ship were thrown off balance, and furniture shot forward across the decks. The height coxswain pulled hard on his wheel in an effort to right the airship, and managed to get her on an even keel once more. Within seconds, however, she plunged down again and this time the cox could do nothing to pull her out of the dive.

The officers in command could see what was coming. They ordered all engines to be cut dead—although in the confusion only one was stopped—and warning bells were rung throughout the airship.

It is difficult to imagine, but there was no panic. Airship flight is normally so smooth and buoyant, and altitude changes so much a part of the pattern, that few people would leap to the idea of 'crashing' in the way that modern aircraft passengers might. The professional men on board were trained to remain calm in dangerous situations; besides, it was just not 'the thing' to panic in front of one's peers. Perhaps also their faith in God and the British Air Ministry held firm.

The chief coxswain had time to go aft, where the crew members were sleeping, to announce quite matter-of-factly, 'We're down, lads.'

With a great grinding noise of engines ceasing and metal grating on metal, the airship lumbered to the earth and slid several yards along the ground.

Then, less than a minute after her last wireless transmission, she exploded into flames. A crashing roar swept through the valley as five million cubic feet of hydrogen ignited.

It shook the nearby village of Allonne to its foundations, and shattered windows. Sheets of flame towered into the sky. The furnace that was once an airship lit up the countryside with a ghastly yellow light, like some nightmarish sun. Night had turned into day.

People in the vicinity of Beauvais were awakened by the thunder. On rushing to their windows, they saw streaks of light soaring across the sky.

Next day, all that could be seen was a massive tangle of scorched metal. The twisted, burnt and charred framework was all that remained of the glorious R.101. She had been completely destroyed by fire. Forty-eight men perished out of a total of fifty-four passengers and crew.

That tragedy finished the British airship industry and was counted among the worst disasters of the twentieth century.

One of those aboard was Squadron Leader William Palstra, M.C., B.A.

This is his story.

PALSTRA FAMILY TREE

Wiebe PALSTRA (b. 4 March 1867 Harlingen, Friesland, Netherlands d. 1944) married **Jacoba Christina Hendrika ENGELBERT VAN BEVERVOORDE** (b. 29 December 1858 Deventer, or Hasselt, Overijssel, Netherlands. d. 1935). Their children:

- William (b. 8 October 1891 Zwolle, Overijssel, Netherlands. d. 5 October 1930, France)
- Henrietta Christina Alberdina (b. 10 October 1892 Amsterdam, Netherlands. d. 23 July 1969 USA?)
- Charles Engelbert (13 January 1893? 94? Amsterdam, Netherlands. d. Australia) Probably born in 1893.
- Frank Elwyn (b. 5 October 1896 St. Jean, Belgium. d. 23 September 1957, Australia)
- Blanche Evangeline (b. 14 October 1898 Brussels, Belgium. d. November 1978 Melbourne, Australia)
- James Victor (b. 26 October 1900 Belgium.)
- John Bernard Philip (b. 7 September 1904 Johannesburg, South Africa. death date unknown, possibly September 24 1957 Australia)

William Palstra in AIF uniform with swagger stick (date unknown)

'Only time, not space, separates us from the past.'

~ Author unknown ~

Recap of The Call to Arms:

The Clerk Who Dared the Great Adventure
VALIANT HEART 2

In *The Call to Arms* (Valiant Heart 1), twenty-two-year-old office clerk Will Palstra travels by steamship to Melbourne, Australia, to join his missionary family, who have been posted there by the Salvation Army.

It is 1914, and war has just been declared. On one side of the conflict are the Central Powers, a coalition consisting of the German Empire and Austria-Hungary; in other words the 'central' European states. The Ottoman Empire (which included Turkey) joined them in 1914, as did Bulgaria in 1915.

On the other side are the Allied Powers, (also called the Allies, or the Entente Powers), formally joined together by the Treaty of London in September, 1914.

They include the United Kingdom of Great Britain and Ireland, the dominions (self-governing colonies) of the British Empire, France, and the Russian Empire. Although the British Crown has run India since 1858, it is not officially a dominion.

Others that would also join the Allies include Portugal, Japan and Italy.[1] At this time British dominions include Canada, New Zealand, South Africa, Newfoundland and Australia.

By the time Will arrives in Melbourne his younger brother Charles, aged 21, has already enlisted in the Australian Imperial Force (AIF).

On the 25th of April 1915, Australian and New Zealand soldiers form part of the Allied expedition that disembarks on the shores of the Gallipoli peninsula in Turkey, and Charles Palstra is one of them. He is wounded at Gallipoli, but survives the carnage—physically, at least.

Back in Melbourne, Will enlists in the AIF on 3 January 1916, at the age of 24. He joins the 39th infantry battalion AIF (Tenth Brigade), which is sent to a training camp at the Victoria town of Ballarat.

In May 2016 he voyages overseas on a troop ship, with the 39th. The men complete their training in England, on Salisbury Plain, in the shadow of Stonehenge. It is here that Will glances up and beholds a biplane soaring overhead—a modern machine not yet seen in Australia. Fired with enthusiasm for flying, Will applies to join the Royal Flying Corps (RFC), but his application is refused. The queue to become an airman is long, and competition is fierce. He will have to prove himself, if he is ever to have a chance of becoming an aviator.

Having displayed initiative and efficiency during training, Will is selected to study for a commission. He and his fellow students spend the bitter winter of 1916-17 in quarters

---

1   Other countries that opposed the Central Powers would come to be called 'Associated Powers,' instead of 'Allied Powers'. When the Americans entered the war in April 1917, President Woodrow Wilson insisted that the USA's autonomy must be preserved by this distinction. At war's end, the 1919 Treaty of Versailles listed 27 'Allied and Associated Powers'. Source: Encyclopaedia Britannica: History & Facts: Allied powers.

at Baliol College, Oxford University, while the rest of the 39th Battalion joins the bloody fighting on the Western Front, in France and Belgium.

Will graduates as a Second Lieutenant, and in April 1917, leading a platoon of reinforcements for the AIF, he crosses the English Channel to the war zone. He has had, as yet, no experience of active duty.

Unbeknownst to him—for it is an official secret—for many months the Allies have been preparing to mount a massive attack on the enemy near the village of Messines in West Flanders, Belgium. And the 39th Battalion, shoulder-to-shoulder with other Allied units, is destined to play a part.

Picture Second Lieutenant Palstra as he makes his way to the front line in 1917, filled with enthusiasm for his new career, and determination to overcome all challenges. Now 25 years old, he is still lean and wiry, but much stronger and fitter than when he was an office clerk. He stands 5 foot 9 inches tall (69 inches or 1.75 metres). His eyes have been labelled 'blue' by the army physicians. His short hair is light brown, and by this date he is sporting a fashionable moustache, like so many other officers.

He is dressed in his khaki uniform, his calves swathed in 'puttees'. The badges of his rank are displayed, on his cuffs or epaulettes—one Bath star or 'pip' for a second lieutenant, with a Tudor crown and the word "AUSTRALIA". His peaked service cap is adorned with the shining Australian Army General Service Badge, better known as the 'Rising Sun' badge. One of these badges is also pinned to his collar.

His cloth colour patches are stitched to the upper sleeves of his khaki tunic. The colours of the 10th Brigade battalions are oval in shape. Each oval is divided in half along the horizontal. The bottom half is filled with the Brigade colour—red for the Tenth. The top is filled with the battalion colour. For the 39th Battalion, it is a dark purplish brown; 'Mud over Blood' as the men of the battalion have come to call the badge; a term of endearment that will, in future days, prove only too appropriate.

Part I: 1917
1. The Western Front

Étaples to Armentières

Prior to embarkation from Australia the men of the AIF had each been issued with a printed pamphlet of guidelines for soldierly behaviour. It read:

1. Don't show the white flag unless your officer orders you to.
2. Don't stop firing or advancing because the enemy shows a white flag till your officer orders you to do so.
3. Don't, however, fire deliberately at the man showing the flag.
4. Don't have any friendly chat with the enemy; he is just as likely to be treacherous as not.

5. Don't kill a man who has thrown his arms down as a sign that he has ceased to resist.
6. Don't be heartbroken if you kill such a one by mistake; it is his fault for having resisted up till too late.
7. Don't fail to shoot a wounded man who continues to fight; he is quite right to do so, but you cannot be expected to treat him differently from a "hale" man.
8. Don't hide your weapons or your uniform.
9. Don't spare an enemy who does the same; haul him to your officer and let him deal with him.
10. Don't rub or file your bullets; if you are caught with such bullets on you, you will be shot, and serve you right.
11. Don't shoot a spy offhand; he is doing a very plucky thing and deserves a trial. All the same, don't let him off, and don't give him time to make up a story.
12. Don't become a prisoner of war if you can help it, they will be getting short rations by June.
13. But, if caught: Don't resist your guards.
14. Don't refuse to work; you have no right to jib at any work except such as is connected with the fighting actually in progress.
15. Don't refuse to give your name and regiment; it doesn't do any good, and your people won't know what has become of you.
16. Don't fail to escape if you get a chance.
17. Don't maltreat prisoners of war when first captured, or take their private property.
18. Don't fail to shoot a prisoner of war who tries to escape.
19. Don't fail to shoot a prisoner of war trying to assist the enemy.
20. Don't fail to shoot a prisoner of war who assaults you viciously.
21. Don't fail to down a prisoner of war who resists you in any other way.

22. Don't torture a prisoner for information.
23. Don't give parole except through your officer.
24. Don't act treacherously or in any way which has a hint of meanness in it.
25. Don't let yourself be caught by the others acting treacherously.
26. Don't be a brute because the enemy is one. If he breaks the laws you may be sure that some suitable punishment will be thought out and inflicted; but, as for yourself,
27. Don't go beyond your rights, and do as you would be done by.'

Will, who took his obligations seriously, would have adhered to the instructions.

Admiralty Pier, Dover. Troops embarking for France, 1917.
Photo courtesy of Dover Museum

Battlefield France

After accompanying their platoons of reinforcements across the channel from England to France, Lieutenant Palstra, accompanied by two of his fellow officer-graduates, reported to the headquarters of Third Division Australian Base Depot in Étaples. There they received further orders to conduct their men to the city of Armentières.

France in 1916-17 was a landscape of stark contrasts; picturesque, medieval villages and chateaux amid fairy-tale forests, juxtaposed with hellish scenes of utter desolation and ruin.

The Western Front, the long line between territory captured by the Germans and territory held by the Allies, stretched right across France. It comprised a series of trenches that ran seven hundred kilometres from the Belgian coast to the Swiss border.

Where once little villages had stood, now lay a sea of mud. The countryside was a howling desolation; it had been torn to pieces by shell-fire and the rain had completed the work of the artillery.

The battle front had ceased to move back and forth, because both sides were finding it hard to advance into enemy territory. As soon as the front became stationery, the Allies had set to work streamlining the system for supplying food, forage, mail, ammunition, equipment and other supplies by building a complex railway system of light rail and tramways running from the Channel ports to the front.

Leading their platoons of reinforcements, Will and his comrades arrived in the French city of Armentières before sunrise on the morning of Tuesday 24th April 1917. The march from Steenwerck had a sobering influence on men of all ranks, especially as they neared their destination. They were heavily laden with equipment and arms, and the country roads were pot-holed, muddy and tortuous. Packs were filled to their utmost capacity, blankets and steel helmets fixed to the outside, and haversacks crammed with iron rations and such oddments of kit as could not be wedged into the packs. It was a tough four-and-a-half-hour march along dark cobbled roads and rutted lanes heading, for the first time, close to the trenches.

They were not permitted to show any lights. Many times along the road, policemen ordered them to halt and stand to one side, to allow the passage of men and guns going up to where the line of constantly bursting star shells and cannon flashes lit the horizon for as far as the eye could see. The boom of guns sounded unpleasantly close as the men entered the city, and on every side they witnessed evidence of the havoc and destruction of war.

Armentières! The name was well-known.

In 1917, that medieval "city of fabric" was an important place in the Allied lines. It lay on a main route to and from the trenches where units were billeted. It was also a depot for support and Lines of Communication troops, Divisional Headquarters for the neighbouring sectors, the site of many artillery gun sites and a forward rail-head for that part of the front.

Before the war, Armentières had been a moderately large manufacturing centre. It was home to numerous large textile factories, and quite a few smaller mills manufacturing paper and flour. There used to be several breweries, too. During the war, some of them were still in operation. It had been quite a busy place, in the days of its prosperity—more than thirty thousand people had lived there.

Things had changed drastically by 1916. Paterson wrote that Armentières was a typical example of the great number of French and Belgian cities over which the ruthless scythe of war had swept, leaving desolation in place of peaceful industry. In 'Somme Mud', EPF Lynch described such cities as 'pulverised brickyards'.

France was taking quite a battering.

Half Past Eleven Square, an open, cobblestoned area surrounded by buildings, was on one of the main routes through the town. The troops in this sector had given it its title in 1914, after a shell struck the town hall's fine old clock tower, causing the clock's hands to be stuck forever at half past eleven.

Paterson noted that Armentières had once been in many respects a beautiful city. It was a quaint, old-world town built almost entirely of red brick. The spires of many fine churches —some of them now badly damaged by shell fire—towered above the houses. A shell had blown off the top of the massive Gothic tower of Notre Dame and blown in the stained-glass windows, "... and yet services still go on daily," wrote Major General John Monash, commander of the Australian 3rd Division, "and my own troops use the church regularly for Divine Service."

In December 1916 he wrote, "... the large town of Armentières ... is close up to my front line, and receives delicate attentions from Fritz every day in the shape of a few 10- and 15-centimetre shells. As a result, only about 5000 out of its usual 30,000 inhabitants are left, and those mostly of the poorer class who are too poor to get away—work people in the local factories.

"Such a scene of desolation as it is would be hard to describe; streets dead and deserted. Rows and rows of two and three storey houses and shops with roofs all gone, and all the windows shattered, often the whole front blown out, with the furniture all exposed as the owners left it. Heaps of debris and bricks lumbering the streets and footpaths. Many houses gutted by fire where the shells have set alight to them..."

It was here in this wrecked city that the 39th Battalion and its brother battalions lived during the intervals between tours of duty in the front line. And it was here that Second Lieutenant Palstra now found himself, in a night that was stabbed by sudden bursts of light on the horizon, and punctuated by the thunder of artillery. Field guns were firing, and searchlights flashing over a distant German parapet.

It was all very "rough and ready". Will recorded:

'23rd [April] Monday Arrived Steenwerke 10 pm. Marched Reinforcements to Armentières arriving at Half Past Eleven Square at 3am. Slept that night 40th Qlb Store.'

WORLD WAR I: Armentières. Main street of Armentières destroyed by battle, France.

Photograph, c1916. Alamy FG76EX

Armentières July 1918. The handwriting is in German. "Frankreich" means "France".

Australian transport passing shell-damaged Notre Dame Church at Armentières in France circa 1917. AWM E02014

Informal portrait of Brigadier General Ramsay McNicoll, commanding the 10th Australian Infantry Brigade, outside his sandbagged Headquarters at Armentières, in France. AWM E00074

On leaving Tenth Brigade Headquarters, the three officers marched the rest of their men through the rubble-strewn streets of Armentières on their way to 39th Battalion Headquarters. Behind the roofless towers of shelled buildings, a few observation balloons probably hung in the sky. These dirigibles, lifted by hot air, were tethered to the ground by strong cables. From the high vantage point they afforded, watchers could gaze out across the landscape into territory held by the enemy.

What a surreal experience it was, to arrive in this French city. Armentières was right up against the front line, but in the city's heart large crowds of soldiers were strolling up and down the Rue de Lille and other main streets, while patisserie and souvenir shops did a roaring trade. Even closer to the fighting, French girls sold the Continental Daily Mail to soldiers in the subsidiary trenches, apparently oblivious to any danger.

Day and night, almost without let-up, white-hot shells arced through the skies and crashed on Armentières. The citizens had become familiar with the bellowing fury of bursting missiles and poison gas. War, to a great extent, had lost its terrors for them. Bizarrely, it seemed, they went about their daily business with a fatalistic shrug of the shoulders and the murmured 'C'est la guerre' ('That's war: it can't be helped') that greeted each fresh misfortune or trial.

The headquarters of the 39th Battalion were situated in the partly-shelled Chateau de la Rose. This mansion, situated across the road from the Houplines Church, occupied spacious and parklike grounds beside the river Lys. It even had a small moat. Its many grand rooms were oak-panelled, and the upper storey boasted a small tower and a turret.

A British soldier recorded that "The inhabitants had left their house and gone to Boulogne leaving a 'domestic' in charge. Most of the smaller furniture had been removed, but such things as the grand piano, tables, chairs, etc., were still in the house."[2]

In February, 1917, Lieutenant-Colonel Henderson had replaced Rankine as the 39th's commanding officer. When Second Lieutenants Palstra, Speering and Ricketts reported to him at the Chateau de la Rose, delivering the reinforcements, he would have congratulated them on their success at Oxford and informed them which platoon to take charge of. Will's was Number 14, in D Company.

Will had arrived in France at a significant time. The war had been going through a period of stalemate, characterised by sniping, periodic shelling and raids, with no strategic advances by either side.

This would soon change.

---

2   From the diary of Sgt Bernard Joseph Brookes, 'Queen's Westminster Rifles' 1914/1915. Diary entry dated 13.1.1915

The newly-arrived officers were informed that the Allies were preparing for a battle that would initiate a serious attempt to push the Germans back. For about eighteen months, Allied commanders had been planning a major attack on Messines Ridge, and it was all coming to a head very soon. The Third Division would be playing a leading role. The plans were fairly 'hush-hush' still of course, because the War Office did not want the enemy to get wind of them, but there were some details all officers should know in advance. They would be briefed about it later.

Meanwhile there was other work to be done. Up till now the 39th Battalion had been stationed in the Houplines sector, holding a section of the front line of established trenches which the men chaffingly called a "nursery section," because there was not much activity there.

2. In the Trenches

It was now time for the 39th Battalion to relieve the 43rd from their stint in the front-line trenches in the dangerous Ploegsteert sector. For the 39th Battalion, Saturday 28th April 1917 passed in a fever of activity. Every man reviewed his orders and checked his battle kit, which contained field glasses, maps, a compass, ammunition, flare pistol, service pistol, a blanket, greatcoat, paybook and identity disks, box respirator, steel helmet, comforter, socks, a holdall, a tin of iron rations, a towel and soap, powder for "trench feet" which had been issued by the quartermaster-sergeant, a mess tin, a 'housewife' (sewing kit), a jack-knife, field dressings, a knife, a fork and a spoon, all wrapped up in a waterproof sheet.

They packed everything into khaki-coloured canvas kit bags with their name, number and unit stencilled on the outside in white paint. A piece of hempen rope through the eyelets in the top allowed closure and doubled as a carry handle. The kit bag was locked with a brass clip. As well there was a loop at the bottom of the bag. This allowed the rope to be put through it forming a sling so that the whole lot could be slung over the shoulder.

The front line trenches

In the Great War, the purpose of the fighting was to capture as much of the enemy's territory as possible, while preventing him from getting yours. "Holding the line" refers to the act of defending the border between your own territory and that of the enemy. That border runs somewhere down the middle of "no-man's-land", a piece of ground that 'belongs' to neither side. Your own front line is the closest point to no-man's-land that is still under the control of your side.

As General Monash explained in his letters, "The front 'line' is not really a line at all, but a very complex and elaborate system of field works, extending back several thousands of yards and bristling with fire trenches, support and communication trenches, redoubts strong points, machine-gun emplacements and an elaborate system of dug-outs, cabins, posts, and observation cells.

"Life in the front system is very arduous and uncomfortable, and a front line battalion stays in only six days, during which each platoon is changed round so that at the worst a single man seldom does more than 48 hours continuous front trench duty in every twelve days, and every 48 days the whole brigade gets relieved by the reserve brigade and goes out for a complete rest, or for work in the back area for a clear 24 days. . ."

The mud of the trenches was famously one of the enemies the men had to wrestle with. "Everything within 2000 yards (1.8km or 1.1 miles) of the front line is just a sea of mud," wrote Monash. "No vehicles or motor cars or cycles can go up closer than 3000 yards (1.7 miles or 2.7 km). . ."

On Saturday 28th April at 9pm, as the sun sank behind the ruins of Armentières. the main part of the 39th Battalion left their billets and moved off in formation through the wilderness of broken bricks and mortar. They were sweating under the burden of their equipment.

The front was quiet and the night still, save for the occasional rattle of a machine gun. Intermittently, star shells soared through the air, illuminating the surroundings vividly for a few moments, then winking out to leave the night blacker than ever. Deep shell holes littered their path. Now and then they passed the swollen body of a dead horse.

After navigating their way through the support lines, the battalion split into companies. An officer's voice, pitched low, came through the darkness: "Lead on, 'D' Company." Lieutenant Palstra's company went ahead for several yards, then halted. Guides from the 43rd, who had been waiting there, led each platoon to their allotted positions on the front line.

A strict mode of procedure governed the relief of a unit in the line. The men of the 43rd Battalion were standing to arms on the fire step of their trench in readiness to hand over, and as the 39th filed in, they lined the parapet alongside the garrison about to be relieved.

Meanwhile the officers commanding companies and platoons—including Will—were making a tour of inspection and taking over such stores as were kept permanently in the trenches.

The word was passed down the line, and the men of the 43rd left their posts. They climbed out of the trenches and filed quietly out of the front line, fading into the night. In their place the 39th slipped and slid into the trenches. There, they shucked off their equipment and loaded their rifles. The relief was completed without any untoward incident, and thus the men of the 39th Battalion found themselves facing enemy lines with only the narrow, ominous strip of no-man's-land between themselves and the Hun.

The entire operation was completed by 11 pm, with no casualties.

Painting of soldiers walking along "Regent Street" duckboard track in Ploegsteert Wood, circa 1917. From The Daily Mirror.

In the dark, the men were conversing in undertones. Each soldier was allotted to a post. Now their job was to watch and wait.

Once Second Lieutenant Palstra had made sure that Number 14 platoon was settled in, he was able to take a closer look at this underground world.

Being a fighting trench, it was about twelve feet (3.7 m) deep. This was a limited, linear world. To either side you could only see along the trench as far as the end of the firebay.

Trenches were never straight. They were deliberately laid out in a zigzag pattern that broke the line into firebays connected by traverses.

Fire-bays were straight sections of trench from which the troops did their shooting.

Traverses were built at angles. This meant that a soldier could never see more than ten yards or so along the trench. It also meant that if the enemy penetrated at any point they could not rake the entire trench with gunfire, and if an explosive device landed in the trench the blast could not travel far. The walls of the trenches were revetted with sandbags, wooden frames and wire mesh. Wooden duckboards covered the floor.

Had Will climbed onto the fire-step and looked through a loophole (a gap in the sandbags) over the parapet, he would have seen the mass of tangled barbed wire, attached to picket posts, that covered the ground between the trench and no- man's-land.

This wicked entanglement was impenetrable. When troops received the signal to attack, officers would send out a party of men with wire cutters to clear a path. The artillery batteries would then shell the enemy's wire and blow a gap in it, so that the troops could charge through to their trenches.

Out there in no-man's-land, corpses lay in twisted positions. Here and there arms and legs and heads protruded from the churned-up morass, where dead men had been partially buried by dirt thrown up by shelling. Through the dimness, streams of rats could be glimpsed scurrying furtively across the ground, occasionally scuttling across the parapet right above the men.

The millions of rats in the trenches and no-man's-land had grown so huge and bold that they could eat a wounded man if he couldn't defend himself. They crawled over, and often bit sleeping troops.

This was a night war. Generally, from sunset till sunrise the pounding of artillery shook the air and the ground.

Accompanied by the thunder and roar of shells, the first day of duty in the trenches began to dawn and the 39th Battalion mounted a gas attack against the enemy. Come full daylight, things got quieter. As the sun rose the bombardment eased off and gradually died down.

The 39th Battalion had received its 'baptism of fire'.

Will with his platoon in the trenches on the Western Front, 1917

A German dugout built in a portion of their front line system immediately before La Douve Farm, near Messines and captured by the 39th Battalion in the Battle of 7 June 1917. The west slope of Messines Ridge and Hill 49 can be seen in the background. The Douve River, which was the dividing line between two German armies, ran along the foot of the slope. AWM E01285

Daily life in the trenches

For Second Lieutenant Palstra and his comrades in the 39th, life in the trenches, once the novelty had faded, followed a daily ordered routine to which they quickly adapted themselves.

Morning:

The day was measured from 'Stand-To' (short for 'Stand-to-Arms'), an hour before dawn, to 'Stand-To' on the following day. No bugler sounded reveille as a wake-up call— that would have attracted the enemy's attention.

During Stand-To, every man stood on the trench fire-step, rifle loaded, bayonet fixed. It was thought that most enemy attacks would be mounted under cover of darkness, either before dawn or shortly after dusk. As a result, both sides made careful preparations at such times, manning the fire-step before dawn and dusk.

"Stand-To lasted between half an hour and an hour, after which each man would be ordered to stand down; breakfast would follow in the morning."

When at last broad daylight washed over the landscape, officers walked along each narrow lane between the high banks of sandbags giving the order, 'Stand Down', whereupon the men dispersed to their dugouts, except for those whose turn it was to be on sentry duty for the first two hours. Enemy snipers made it too dangerous to put one's head over the parapet in daylight, and besides, to do so would betray the position of the post.

A party of carriers would come staggering along the trenches bearing heavy canisters on their backs. The men held out their dixies while hot tea or rum was poured into them.

Sometimes this ritual would be interrupted by the wail and crash of shellfire, whereupon the men crouched low in the trench, bracing their backs against the parapet for a few minutes until the enemy's "morning hate" had passed.

Army fare on the front line proved to be as monotonous and lacking in freshness as foretold. It consisted mainly of bread, hard biscuits known as 'Anzac wafers', bully beef (tinned corned beef) prepared in a variety of ways, rice, the occasional rasher of bacon, a little cheese, and jam or marmalade. Sometimes there would be tinned custard. Since no refrigeration was available, rations were preserved by canning, pickling or drying, or by the addition of salt or sugar. Families sent parcels of food from home, and the men scrounged extras when they could. Officers' rations included whisky, which was not permitted to 'other ranks'. This was wasted on Second Lieutenant Palstra who, with his Salvation Army background, never touched it.

Breakfast could be heated up on the pocket-sized solid-fuel stoves known as 'Tommy Cookers', infamous for their inefficiency. While the men waited for the stove to infuse their food with a tepid warmth, they cleaned their rifles, unclogging the barrel with the 'pull- through', and scraping the mud off the outside of the weapon. The Lewis gunners and bombers were busy checking that their respective weapons were in working order.

After the morning meal, many of the men smoked an 'issue' cigarette, which was also wasted on Second Lieutenant Palstra, but which many of the men pronounced "an indispensable item affording a great deal of satisfaction."

As the sky paled over the front line trenches, the men circulated reports about what had happened during the night. Perhaps a scout had been cut down by a machine gun in front of the wire, or a member of a wiring party had been wounded.

Hygiene:

After breakfast the batmen would wash the officers' dixies. The "other ranks" had to clean their own. The water in the shell-holes was too dirty for washing eating utensils, but the men saved a drop of tea in the bottom of their dixies, and with that, aided by a shred of sandbag or paper, they rinsed them out.

When it was time for daily personal ablutions, sometimes a batman was able to scavenge some luke-warm tea for an officer's use. The men would search for some relatively clean water lying in the bottom of shell holes and trenches. They scooped it up with a 'Maconochie' tin (which had contained a ration of canned stew) or an old steel helmet, which would be used as a washing basin. When the helmet was filled, they would rummage in their haversacks to find their pocket mirror, towel, and soap. Those who felt particularly energetic even had a shave, if the water was not too foul. The officers made sure their platoons also attended to their feet.

Another part of the daily cleanliness routine was inspecting one's clothing for parasites. The men would take off their shirts and singlets, then don their cardigan jackets and tunics to keep warm while each checked his undergarments for lice. Often they would become quite enthusiastic about the hunt.

After the morning ablutions, the sergeants would set the men to work on jobs that did not involve too much moving about. Men were needed to make wire 'gooseberries'—barbed wire reels, named after the prickly fruit—or 'knife-rests'—portable barbed wire entanglement, stretched on X-shaped frames and employed for stopping gaps—ready to use at night for building up the parapet or wiring in no-man's-land.

Noon:

In "Somme Mud", Private Lynch wrote, "Midday finds the trench deserted. The men are curled up in the dugouts sleeping. Afternoon sees a few wandering, yarning, arguing or small parties playing poker or rummy. Or two-up. Others are letter writing; others sleep on, oblivious to all.

"Some of the new reinforcements wander up and down the support trenches—they have collected old Fritz bayonets, a few pounds of shrapnel pellets, nose caps of shells, flattened Fritz copper-clad machine gun bullets and all kinds of useless stuff. I tell them to throw it away."

Around noon every day the men in the trenches fired up the Tommy Cookers again and heated water to brew tea. One of the men would relieve the sentry at the periscope. As often as not, just as the platoon was preparing to eat their "dry rations" of bread and jam and cheese, the enemy would start strafing the trenches. It was not unusual for shells to explode close by, showering the food and drink with clods of dirt as the men tried to dodge the falling debris.

Once or twice, as the men were finishing an after-meal smoke, their attention was drawn by a droning noise in the sky. On looking up they spotted a squadron of German aeroplanes flying overhead. Further off, a couple of Allied scout aeroplanes was disappearing from view, their pilots fully aware that their machines were no match for the German planes, while to the rear of the trenches, Allied anti-aircraft guns rattled loudly to life.

Afternoon:

Customarily, from mid-day till dusk, the trench would continue to appear empty. Men in the front line needed to sleep, so they removed their equipment and greatcoats, grabbed a blanket and crawled into the confined space of a dugout. They left their equipment at the shelter's entrance, because there was no room for it inside. The floor of these dismal holes in the ground were usually about a foot above the duck-board walks, to allow drainage, and the ceilings were only about two feet (60 cm) above the floor.

Having inserted his body, a man continued, with much wriggling in the narrow space to rid his feet of his gumboots, leaving them just outside the dugout with the tops turned down, so that they would not fill with water from rain or drips. This was not easy, because there was no room to sit up. Finally he rolled himself up in his blanket and dragged his greatcoat over him, keeping the muddy side on top. He was now prepared for the sleep he so badly needed and usually would not move until he was roused for tea.

Dusk:

About an hour before dark the men would heat up and consume the evening meal, after which they began to make preparations for the night, and all the "hate" it would bring. When twilight thickened to the extent that the enemy's line was barely visible, the "Stand-To" commenced.

Again, no bugle sounded. Instead, the post commander or the trench sergeant or another NCO would put his head into the cramped dugouts where men were sleeping and call out, "Come on chaps, Stand-To!"

Men would crawl wearily out of the dusty holes in the trench walls, put on their equipment, respirators, and steel helmets and grab their rifles. Then they plodded along the dirty, broken duckboards, often stumbling into muddy shell-holes in the gathering dusk, until their reached their posts a few yards away. Half a dozen men, a section, would gather at each post. There they would stand, peering out across no-man's-land, knowing that beyond the barbed wire the enemy was probably conducting a similar routine. Flares played across the softly brightening horizon, and bursts of machine gun fire erupted sporadically. In the half- light, blasted tree stumps could take on the look of crouching enemy troops.

The entire trench garrison stood at its posts with their rifles and Lewis guns until it was quite dark, and the order to "Stand Down" was passed along the line.

Throughout the daylight hours, when snipers could see clearly, the men had kept quiet and travelled about as little as possible. Now, under cover of darkness the trenches came alive with movement. Working parties were busy with all kinds of repairs, and carrying parties went back and forth with duck-boards and wire, the material for the night's work. There were many tasks to be done, ranging from repairing a bomb-shattered trench to excavating dugouts, laying duck-boards, pumping out water, filling sand-bags, replacing dislodged sandbags or cleaning bombs. Working in the mud and filth, the men cursed at everything and everybody connected with the war.

The scouts were starting out on their dangerous missions to no-man's-land. Perhaps a sergeant and five scouts would come to Second Lieutenant Palstra's post wearing cap-comforters instead of steel helmets, and with the butts of revolvers poking out of their respirators. They would throw away their lighted cigarettes and climb over the parapet, before disappearing through the wire.

Night:

Night sentries were posted. The sunless hours were the most arduous. In the darkness of those cold nights, patrols from both sides crept about no-man's-land as soundlessly as possible, and on many nights the battalion sent out raids against the enemy. Under cover of darkness, also, working parties had to be organised and sent out to repair wires broken by shell fire. Night in the trenches held a multitude of sinister possibilities, and from dusk to dawn everybody in the front line was in a state of preparedness for any eventuality.

Having found some Hales grenades for Platoon No 14, Second Lieutenant Palstra organised little barrages on the enemy front line, resulting in counter bombardment with the hand grenades known popularly as "pine apples".

As mentioned, he also went on night patrols into no-man's-land, where enemy machine gun posts and snipers made patrol work a very risky business. On May 6th, he went out at one o'clock in the morning with four scouts on patrol in no-man's-land. They returned at 1.40 am. The same patrol (comprising different men), on going out again at 2 am, was surprised by an enemy patrol lying in wait behind a hedge, who fired on them. Private Cameron, the patrol leader, was killed, and two men were wounded. It could easily have been Will who accompanied the unlucky second party. This close shave rattled him sufficiently that he made a note of it in his diary.

All the men were obliged to keep a war diary, but Will's entries were always succinct, containing only the bare facts, never embroidered by observations or feelings. He only poured out his inner life in letters to his parents, and even then he "sanitised" his experiences to spare them worry.

By contrast, Private Lynch's first-hand accounts are graphic. His vivid descriptions of trench warfare in Somme Mud give us a better idea of Will's experiences. The book is recommended reading for anyone who would like to know more.

Baths:

It was not until his self-training was completed to his satisfaction that Will permitted himself to go and get a much-desired scrubbing with hot water. He desperately needed to wash off the filth and parasites of the trenches, and get into clean clothes. Two days after the relief of the 39th, he obtained a leave pass and went to Pont de Nieppe to take a bath.

One of the greatest scourges of the troops occupying the Western Front was lice. To add to the discomfort of itching, biting insects, the men became caked with mud—not to mention excrement and other bodily fluids thrown up by explosions—when they were in the trenches.

Pont de Nieppe—or 'Ponty Neep' as the visiting troops called it—was a village some three miles from Touquet Berthe within the Allied lines. There, the British army had rented some premises and established Divisional Baths in what various eye-witnesses described as either an abandoned brewery or dye works, or a disused bleach-works on the banks of the river Lys.

The boilers were huge, keeping the baths and laundries well supplied with hot water. The baths staff would take the dirty clothes from the men each week, have them thoroughly washed, ironed, mended and disinfested of lice, and re-issue them the following week.

The garments, of course, changed owners, but that was a minor consideration. The socks Mum had so lovingly knitted for Will and posted all the way from Australia would end up on someone else's feet. He might end up with army issue, or socks knitted by someone else's mother. But he'd never breathe a word of the exchange to his own Mum.

Monash: "I employ over 200 girls in the laundries washing and ironing the soiled clothes. It is quite a show sight, but how they live and work all day in steam so thick that they can't see 6ft. in front of them I don't know. It's a fine sight to see, the boys splashing about in the great beer vats. They come out looking nice and pink. I have a medical officer in charge of each bath, with a small staff to help him. My pioneers work the boilers, as firemen and stokers."

The Pont de Nieppe baths were also equipped with hydro-extractors and rotary driers, hydraulic presses and huge drying rooms.

A letter[3] from a soldier signing himself as "Digger" describes the baths from first-hand experience:

"In one of the large factories (I believe they were dye works) there were a number of large vats, and in order to combat the lice and other pests with which we became inflicted we were treated to medicated baths in these each time we came out of the trenches. The place used to be crowded with soldiers and in each vat a dozen or more would be bathing at once. We used to march to the baths in a filthy condition, but return with clean underclothing and refreshed bodies. It was a splendid effort of the authorities to keep the men clean and fit."

---

3   Northern Territory Times and Gazette (Darwin, NT: 1873—1927) Saturday 6 March 1920 Page 1

Regimental baths on the Western Front. Image from pikabu.ru, first found on Jan 6, 2017

Regimental laundry. Image from: thesciencebookstore.com. First found on Dec 12, 2013

A French woman serves coffee to Australian and Scottish soldiers at an estaminet (small cafe) in her village, within 800 yards of the trenches in a comparatively quiet sector of the Western Front. AWM EZ0032

3. Magnum Opus

Plans for "Magnum Opus".

By June 1917, something big was brewing on the Western Front. The Third Australian Division was on the eve of its first major conflict.

Field Marshal Haig was a senior officer of the British Army who commanded the British Expeditionary Force on the Western Front. He had long planned a major offensive in the Ypres salient in Flanders—the Third Battle of Ypres, it was to be called.

As a preliminary to this, he ordered General Plumer and his Second Army (the enormous British Expeditionary Force had been split in two for administrative purposes) to take the Messines-Wytschaete Ridge by June, 1917.

Situated southeast of Ypres, the ridge (which the English-speaking troops nicknamed Messines-Whitesheet) was a natural stronghold. The high ground gave the Germans a clear view over the whole Ypres (which the troops called 'Wipers') salient. It was the key to that part of the front. As long as the enemy kept hold of it, they could see every move made by the Allies. That made Ypres the most dangerous part of the front. The sooner the enemy was removed from Messines Ridge the better, as far as the Allies were concerned. If they could seize that strategic high ground, they would be one step closer to victory.

The enemy's defensive positions were enormously strong. The whole town of Messines, though a complete wreck, was nothing less than a fortress of concrete machine-gun posts; an extremely difficult obstacle for attacking infantry to face. The Germans had held and fortified it since 1914, and such robust defences demanded a new assault strategy, with a huge amount of preparation.

For more than eighteen months, the Allies had been preparing for the Battle of Messines. In January 1916, companies of Canadian, Australian, New Zealand and British engineers began tunnelling beneath the German lines, along the flank of Messines Ridge.[4]

The tunnels, or 'saps', had to be deep enough to avoid the gelatinous sludge of the waterlogged Flanders subsoil, to minimise risk from mortar-fire and to reduce the danger of dislodging enemy mines that had been buried closer to the surface. The greater depth would also deaden the sounds of digging. They had to be dug through a deep stratum of blue clay, a difficult layer. The German sappers, thwarted by the clay, in most cases failed to discover the tunnelling work that was going on at that depth and instead sought the British mining systems closer to the surface.

General Plumer authorised the laying of twenty-two gigantic explosive-packed land mines deep in those tunnels, between Hill 60 in the north and St. Yves in the south, his plan being to detonate them simultaneously, at "zero hour"—a precise moment which was kept a closely guarded secret in case the knowledge fell into enemy hands—on 7th June 1917. The explosions were to be followed immediately by infantry attacks on the German defenders while they were still shocked and confused. In their assault on the ridge, the infantry were to be strongly supported by artillery bombardments, tanks and the use of gas.

---

4   Their efforts are commemorated in at least two motion pictures—"The War Below" (2021) and "Beneath Hill 60" (2010).

Despite German counter-mining, by June 7th 1917 eight thousand metres of hidden galleries had been constructed beneath the German front and 454,000 kilograms (one million pounds) of ammonal laid in the sap-heads. This was enough explosive to reduce the enemy's almost impenetrable fortifications to rubble, and to shatter the Messines front line defences.

All the while the Allies were on edge in case the enemy discovered the plan. They knew that the Germans were suspicious and that they would question captured prisoners. For this reason the finer details of the offensive were not revealed to the rank and file until the last possible moment.

It was while the 39th Battalion was manning the front-line trenches that their Commanding Officer was informed of the precise role the Third Division would play in this conflict. The opening attack on Messines Ridge, which was to take place on 7th June, was code-named "Magnum Opus". Unofficially it was also called "the grand advance" or "the big push".

The Germans, having witnessed many of the above-ground preparations for Magnum Opus from their positions high on Messines Ridge, guessed that an assault was about to be launched. Daily, they brought increasingly heavy artillery fire to bear on the Allied lines and back areas in a desperate attempt to break up their concentrations of men, guns and materiel.

Meanwhile the Allies continued to work furiously on the final preparations for the forthcoming assault.

Will's diary, 27th May 1917:

"Preparation for the Grand Advance well in hand. All work such as assembly, communication, jumping off etc. trenches to be finished by June 2nd. Officers take it in turn to supervise working parties. On the whole a lazy life, enlivened occasionally by the uncomfortably close bursting of a shell."

In the skies over the Western Front, extraordinary activity on the part of the British fighting and scouting planes also hinted at approaching battle. Every day, squadrons of RFC planes patrolled up and down the front line, ready to pounce upon and destroy any enemy who ventured to cross.

In spite of the enemy's hammering, by June 6th, all arrangements for the attack on Messines Ridge were in place.

Nine infantry divisions were to attack on a front of about 17,000 yards, an average of 1,900 yards to each division. The 39th battalion had orders to cross Ulrica Trench and its supports, clearing out any enemy that had survived the explosions. They were then to spread out and "consolidate", making sure they had joined up with other battalions and companies along their objective— the "Black Line"—on each flank, with no gaps. This Black Line was simply a mark drawn on a map, along the eastern crest of Messines Ridge.

The specific task of Second Lieutenant Palstra's platoon, Number 14, was to carry out a flank attack on an enemy stronghold known as Grey Farm. This ruin, a few low piles of bricks splashed with white mortar dust, was known to contain German shelters. It lay immediately behind the front trench of the German second line ("Ulster Reserve") and was screened by a thin hedge. This attack was intended as a diversion, the task of capturing the place being the responsibility of the battalion on their right.

The men of the Third Division were eager to fight, eager to be tried, and to prove their mettle. Every man was ready for the battle and equipped with the regulation supply of ammunition, bombs, iron rations—tins of bully beef and biscuits—a pick or shovel, field dressing, water bottle, sandbags, rifle, bayonet and gas mask.

To facilitate re-organisation during the action, the men of each company wore distinctive colour patches sewn on to the backs of their tunics. Second Lieutenant Palstra's batman had stitched on his pink destination patch. On the eve of battle, it was Will's job to check that each man of 14 Platoon had attached a pink patch to his uniform, to indicate that his goal was to reach an enemy stronghold at an area known as Grey Farm, via a trench called Ulrica Lane.

Runners were constantly coming up to the officers, delivering streams of messages handwritten on standard army forms. At about 4 pm on 6 June, Will and his fellow officers received a coded message which proved to be a Second Army message from General Plumer giving zero hour as 3.10 am, and wishing the 39th Battalion God's speed.

"Zero hour" had finally been revealed.

A little later Second Lieutenant Palstra received another message, which he folded and tucked into his pocket. It was one of many messages typed on pale yellow notepaper, that would end up in the family archives a century later.

Army form C, 2128 "C" Form

MESSAGES AND SIGNALS

To: G.C.D. Coy

Sender's Number: L.L.B. Day of Month: 6.6.17 Lieutenant Palstra orderly officer will supervise and check time of starting of approach march.

See operative orders.

From: L.L. Beauchamp Lt., Adjutant. Time: 5.5 pm.

In a field near the farm late that afternoon, one of the Brigade's padres gathered the men together and held a communion service for those who were about to go into battle. Later, the company commander spoke to the officers.

From Will's diary:

"6.6.17 9 pm Lt Colonel Henderson calls the officers together wishing us all God's speed in this our first big affair. He shakes each officer by the hand commencing with me. Wrote a last letter home and gave it to Roberts in case I fell." (Roberts was probably Will's batman).

"In case I fell". Four words that reveal the extraordinary courage of Will and his comrades. They had no idea whether this was to be their last day of life, yet they did not flinch from the danger.

General Plumer made the following famous remark to his staff the evening before the attack on Messines Ridge: "Gentlemen, we may not make history tomorrow, but we shall certainly change the geography."

Just before midnight, the infantry began their approach march.

The approach march

Under cover of darkness on June 6th, the eight attack-battalions of the Third Australian Division silently left their several camps and their billets. Shells wailed and crumped along the Western Front, guns boomed, and as ever the horizon flickered, alive with flames and coloured lights.

Second Lieutenant Palstra, leading 14 Platoon, made sure that he kept himself at a distance of twenty-five yards behind the tail end of 13 Platoon. He could discern the men up ahead, moving through moonlight and shadows with barely a sound. More than two thousand infantrymen were making their way in columns of fours on dark roads beside moving wheel and motor traffic. Each man had his battle-order equipment on, bayonet fixed to his rifle.

Each had a sandbag of Mills bombs slung in front with the neck of the bag turned back to give ready access to the grenades. Every third or fourth man carried a pair of wire cutters to cut any of the enemy's barbed wire that the shellfire had missed. Every second man had a spade shoved down his back and all had half a dozen empty sandbags jammed through their equipment somewhere.

All the men were on edge. During the critical hours of the approach march the one thought which was uppermost in every man's mind was preoccupying the minds of all the others: does the enemy know?

At midnight, when Will's company—D Company—was still about three quarters of a mile from Oosthove, they heard the soft pat-pat of exploding shells, falling like the scattered heavy drops before a thunder-shower. They had run right into a gas shell bombardment directed against the approaches to the Allied trenches. It was a lethal combination of tear gas, chlorine and phosgene and high explosive.

Poison gas attack. French army attacking from front line trenches circa 1917.
Image from www.maristen-gymnasium.de. First found on Apr 23, 2008

"Respirators on!" Almost before the words had left Will's lips his men had pulled their box respirators, or "gas masks", over their heads.

They now resembled beings from some alien world. The fabric covered their faces completely. With difficulty they peered through circular eye-holes of amber-tinted glass. Tubular nose-pieces stuck out in front of each gas-mask, from which a ribbed hose about two feet in length ran to a tin, strapped to the wearer's body. This contained material to filter the poisons out of the air.

The box respirators protected the wearers from being gassed, but always caused problems if they had to undertake heavy labour. The filtration systems struggled to deal with a heavy demand for fresh air.

This made the remainder of the platoon's march to Annscroft Avenue one long drawn-out misery.

"Between our billets and the front line," wrote Will, "we went through the most awful experience I ever want to go through. All the way up we were shelled with asphyxiating, and lachrymatory gas shells, high explosive and shrapnel. We had to wear gas masks, it was pitch dark, we fell into huge shell holes, streams, and ran into briars. It was hell."

Due to the mere effort of marching under the load of rifle, ammunition, tools, and rations, and the excitement of the occasion, every man was breathing heavily. The masks clung stiflingly around the wearers' faces, causing enormous distress as they gasped for breath. The platoons of the 39th passed harnessed horses and mules foundering on the road, gasping piteously in the poisonous air.

Second Lieutenant Palstra felt the burden of fighting equipment pressing like a deadweight on his shoulders. He could barely see through the darkness, the gaseous haze and the film of sweat and mud smeared across his eye pieces. The other men in the column were similarly half blind. Their pace slowed.

Screaming and thundering, high explosive shells were crashing all around, in a leaping, flashing, burning roar of brilliant light. Enemy flares opened overhead like comets. A nearby explosion lifted several men into the air. When they fell, they did not move.

"Press on, Fourteen!" Will's voice was muffled by his gas-mask, but he dared not take it off. Overhead, the sky seemed to split as huge black shrapnel shells exploded. Men screamed as red-hot metal fragments hit them. Others stumbled into the great shell holes that abounded, and were gassed as their masks slipped.

On their entering Ploegsteert Wood, in whose stagnant air the poisonous vapours lay densely, the difficulties increased. The night was dark and calm, and the gas hung about like a heavy fog, while the shells came across in a steady stream. Guessing that a major assault was imminent, the Germans were shelling the wood more heavily, using high-explosive and incendiary shells as well.

The men groped their way along the narrow tracks, frequently falling over unseen obstacles into ditches and the great shell holes that abounded, often losing the gas masks from their faces in the fall, or being gassed as their masks slipped. Visibility was so poor that they had to hold onto the bayonet scabbards of their comrades in front to avoid being separated from their units. Long stoppages occurred, intervals of tense anxiety.

Here and there officers and men were hit directly by gas-shells. Their bodies crumpled.

They died before they had even reached the front line on the eve of their first battle. Wherever such incidents dislocated the slowly-moving columns and caused men to rush about in panic, many were gassed by the steady shower of shells. They fell out by the wayside, retching, and collapsed on the ground.

That march to the trenches was like a nightmare. For Will, those hours were more unnerving than any experience in the three-days' battle which followed. The night was fairly dark, his respirator eye-pieces were continually becoming fogged with perspiration, and he kept tripping over obstacles such as barbed wire and groaning men.

Grimly he held on to his gas-mask with one hand. With every step, his feet felt for solid ground, aware that to stumble and lose the mask could be fatal. He could only hope that the random shower of shells would somehow miss him.

The bombardment took a terrible toll. Scores of men were falling out, gassed, or wounded by the flying shell splinters.

Resolutely, Will trudged on.

It was practically impossible for officers and NCOs to wear their masks effectively owing to the necessity of directing and controlling the men.

Far ahead of Second Lieutenant Palstra, at the forefront of the column, Major Tucker, who was leading the battalion, could not see well enough to find his way. He took the risk of pulling down his gas-mask to expose his eyes, retaining only the mouth-piece between his teeth, and the clips on his nostrils. Soon he was overcome by gas.

There being no other company commanders left, Captain Paterson of D Company took command, finding himself the senior officer even before the battle had commenced. Officers and men were overcome every few yards, and the track of the 39th Battalion through Bunhill Row and Mud Lane was strewn with prostrate officers and men coughing and gasping in agony, who had collapsed in the effort to keep the movement going.

At the junction of Mud Lane and the Breastworks the gas zone ended and the men were able to take their respirators off. It was only then that Will could see what havoc had been played with the 39th Battalion.

Here congregated a mixed rabble of all platoons, hopelessly confused, and almost utterly spent and weary. Men were half sobbing, and everywhere dropping with fatigue.

Less than half of Will's platoon remained: three Fighting Section, one Rifle Grenadier, two Bombers, and three Lewis Gunners without the gun. His heart sank, especially at the loss of the gun.

The rest of the battalion had fared equally badly.

The men were sweating profusely, and desperately thirsty, but Second Lieutenant Palstra had to ensure that no one drank from his water bottle until the approach march was over, as per orders.

He passed from man to man, encouraging them and telling them they'd done well. As he had heard other officers do, he scoffed at the enemy. "I promise you, lads," he added, to fire the men up, "that we'll soon enjoy taking our revenge for the gas attack."

Just as they were moving off again young Aisbett, No. 2 on Fourteen Platoon's gun, came staggering up with the weapon, sinking down with exhaustion on learning he had regained his unit. Will could almost have embraced him.

"Well done, Aisbett," he probably said. "Very well done indeed. Good man."

Aisbett had only just turned twenty.

By about 2.20 am most of the men of the 39th who were still standing had reached the Regimental Aid Post at Anscroft Avenue. There, Captain Paterson obtained all available ammonia capsules5 from the Regimental Medical Officer and distributed them among the partially-gassed men.

The battalion pressed on. Grass sprouted underfoot, and a few bushes survived among the scattered shell holes. They reached the Front Line and from there proceeded to the left, arriving in position at 1.50 a.m.

"By the time we reached the front line," recorded Will, "the Battalion had lost more than half its men through this ordeal, and the remainder were absolutely exhausted. They just lay down in the trench and could not move."

The assembly trenches, being situated on high ground, were free from gas. During the short period before zero hour the men were able to recover from the exhaustion of the march. Will bade his platoon remove all their equipment and stretch themselves out flat on the duckboards. It had taken them five and a half hours to cover the five miles to the front line, and the men were exhausted—some of them, the younger ones, almost hysterical.

They lay like dead men.

At 2.10 a white parachute flare floated high over the southern flank—a sign that the time was 'zero minus one hour'. Second Lieutenant Palstra noted it and checked his watch. It was keeping time perfectly. An aeroplane roared low overhead. The Allied onlookers were expecting it and knew that its presence was solely intended to drown the noise of their approaching tanks.

Still the enemy gave no sign of alarm. Clearly he was not aware that in an hour's time nineteen great mines beneath him would be exploded, so careful had the British sappers been to hide traces of their tunnelling operations.

---

5   Ammonia can render chlorine gas relatively harmless. Urine-soaked handkerchiefs were among the earliest defences against chlorine gas, due to the urea in urine, which can break down into ammonia.

The British barrage ceased. The quietness that descended over the Allied forward positions was almost unnerving. In the trenches where Will and his platoon sheltered, all that could be heard was the drone of the night-flying plane and intermittent bark of the British 18- pounders to drown any noise the assembly of infantry and tanks might take. Flares rose and fell as usual on the horizon. In the assembly trenches the men's nerves stretched to the limit as they waited in the uncanny stillness for the opening of the barrage, which would give the signal to attack.

Forty minutes rest to troops in good condition, however, did much to revive their spirits. Those who had the stomach for it partook of some of their rations for breakfast. They drank gratefully from their water bottles.

"Drink sparingly!" Will cautioned. "It might be a long time till we get any more."

Many were sitting up, whispering to one another. Some were checking their watches. He glanced at his own watch. The time was 3.05. Five minutes to zero hour! He roused his boys, and they helped each other on with their equipment as the first tinge of dawn appeared over Messines.

It was the morning of 7th June.

Zero Hour

Second Lieutenant Palstra passed a whisper along the trench. "Three minutes to zero hour—get ready!" He grasped the parapet. Beside him, up and down the length of the trench, the first line of men did the same. The second line, behind them, placed their hands beneath the feet of the first, ready to boost them as they sprang over the top into no-man's-land when the moment came.

At 3.09 unbroken silence reigned.

Will glanced sideways at the pale faces of his men. Beads of sweat stood out on their foreheads and their jaws were clenched, or quivering. Some adjusted the straps of their equipment, though they had already done so many times.

Standing tensely with his hands on the sandbagged parapet, he fixed his eyes on his watch. Only seconds to go. . .

Experiments conducted by the British had shown that after a mine exploded, the thrown-up debris of dirt and rocks would fall to the ground within twenty seconds, and would not endanger unsheltered troops more than 200 yards away. It was hoped that by careful synchronisation of watches, the mines could be fired within ten seconds of one another.

Will waited. The last few moments ticked away. And then, zero hour.

GD Mitchell, in "Backs to the Wall" vividly described what happened: "At 3.10 the tremendous crash of a hundred artillery batteries blazed into action in one awful, all-shattering roar of explosion. Every British battery on the front was in action. Guns flashed from Armentières to Ypres and rivers of machine gun fire poured forth, as the trench walls rocked.

"To the left, near Wytschaete, a huge bubble was swelling, mushroom-shaped, from the earth. It burst, in a thunderous explosion, casting a molten, rosy glow on the under-surface of the dense clouds hanging low above it.

"As its brilliance faded two more bubbles burst beside it. During twenty seconds the same thing happened again and again, from the right to the far left. Underneath the German positions along the ridge, the nineteen great mines had been exploded.

"It seemed as if the Messines Ridge got up and shook itself. All along its flank belched rows of mushroom-shaped masses of debris, flung high into the air. A few seconds later the watchers felt the shocks and heard the rumble of an earthquake."

"In a second—a twinkling of an eye—the enemy lines across the intervening space of no-man's-land broke into one long seething flame of white-hot, bursting steel. The waiting infantry were witnessing the most gigantic and at the same time chillingly spectacular firework that ever had been lit in Flanders, as if the whole southeast were spewing fire.

Great billows of scarlet flame erupted along the German front and the entire landscape was a dancing, flashing glow of jumping light.

"The ground leapt beneath us again and again. Nineteen great mines, thousand tons of explosives gone up. Rockets flared and spread.

"The belly of a low hung cloud reddened to a red glare. Such a glow do you sometimes see when bush-fires, gale-driven devour a dense forest. That glare brightened, faded, and was gone.

"We knew it to be the funeral pyre of complete battalions."

When the British mines laid under the Messines Ridge near Ypres were exploded on June 7th, 1917, they not only changed the landscape, but their noise was so violent that it could also be heard as far away as Dublin, Ireland. It was the loudest man-made sound in history. About 10,000 German soldiers died instantly in the blast.

Of course, this was the signal to attack.

"Come on!" roared Will. He was first to jump over the parapet. Close at his heels his men 'hopped over', out of the trench and into the open.

"I led my boys in single file through our own wire into the centre of no-man's-land, where I proceeded to form them up in some order of battle."

He lined them up—six Lewis Gunners with their Gun, one Rifle Grenadier, two Bombers, three Fighting Section—total, twelve.

All that was left from a platoon of forty-two.

For the moment, they were protected by British artillery fire, which had resumed at the same moment as the explosion of the mines.

G.D. Mitchell in "Backs to the Wall" wrote, "Altogether the guns opened, stunning comprehension. The greatest artillery fire of all time. Swelling and roaring, it climbed up and up to climax beyond incredible climax. Waves of sound beat about us in the madness of vibration. All past standards of measurement were useless.

"We rather took pride in the fact that we could stand calm and upright in the bedlam, that we were prepared to move forward into the storm with stoic indifference. We watched a while. The flame spears leaped undiminished from the ground. Earth and sky still shuddered before the blasts of sound."

Most of the British 18-pounder field guns fired a creeping barrage of shrapnel immediately ahead of the infantry advance, while the other field guns and 4.5-inch Howitzers fired a standing barrage some 700 yards further ahead. As each objective was taken by the infantry, the creeping barrage paused 150 to 300 yards ahead of them and became a standing barrage, protecting the newly-gained positions from counterattack while the infantry consolidated.

"The stream of our machine gun fire," Will recalled vividly, "was like an overpowering Niagara of many waters. And the guns—big guns, small guns, Howitzers, and trench mortars made the ground in front of us one sheet of flame."

14 Platoon was supposed to be part of the second wave of assault, and their objective was that place called 'Grey Farm', or rather to the left of Grey Farm near La Douve River. Grey Farm itself was the objective of the 36th Battalion, 9th Brigade, on their right, and Will's orders were to assist in its capture by a flanking attack on the left.

Here they were then, lined up in the barbed wire tangle of no-man's-land, with every imaginable kind of projectile tearing overhead on its way to the Hun lines. Right now, a first wave of troops should be rushing forward to take the first objective. Will waited for signs of it—one minute—two minutes—nothing appeared.

"As I was the second wave for the furthest objective, I had to wait for the first wave to get started, but the gas shell attack had been too much, there was no first wave."

The British barrage, a truly spectacular affair, was already creeping forward, as planned. If 14 Platoon did not press on, the attack by the flanking battalion would fail, ". . . and," Will explained, "this would perhaps make the whole of the effort futile. For a moment the words of that old pagan Horatius came to me—'How can men die better than by facing fearful odds for the ashes of their fathers and the temples of their Gods?'"

Second Lieutenant Palstra made up his mind quickly. This was no time to dawdle.

Death waited on the other side of no-man's-land. If that was to be their fate, he thought, then it would be an honourable death. There was only one appropriate course of action—he must lead the remnant of the platoon into the attack, regardless of the fact that they were few in number and lacked support.

They would go over in one line and mop up as best they could while advancing. "Prepare to attack. Spread out!" he yelled, gesturing to his men.

Perhaps faces broke into grim smiles as the men moved apart in an effort to cover the ground that ought to have been occupied by four times their number. They were itching to get revenge for their fallen comrades, and could hardly wait to wreak havoc on the enemy.

Fearing to wait any longer for the first wave, Will placed himself ten yards in front of this sparse line and without apparent support on either flank, gave the sign (commands were out of the question—the noise was deafening), for the 'advance'.

"To make yourself heard was impossible, to see where you were going equally out of the question. I had taken the general direction before setting out, and I went forward blindly on this."

The mine explosions, combined with the most tremendous barrage ever, had kicked up churning clouds of dust. Visibility was limited, so the blanket of creamy dust served as a perfect screen as the 39th Battalion rushed forward. To their left and the right, the men of the 40th Battalion and the 9th Brigade could be glimpsed, indistinct figures charging through the murk, bayonets at the ready.

Shells flashed and flamed through the dust and smoke, which was streaked with the flying red and green lights of SOS rockets. Hundreds of British shells were flying past overhead with a swish and a sigh and a violent rush of air. They exploded with tremendous crashes in the enemy trenches, which writhed and seethed in the flaming inferno. No enemy machine gun or rifle fire was punching back at the charging men through the curtain of falling shells. The local German garrison, already overstrained by the week's bombardment, must have been entirely unstrung by the mine explosions.

Amid the indescribable turmoil, dominated by the sharp crack of thousands of British machine gun bullets passing over their heads, the remnants of 14 Platoon, led by Second Lieutenant Palstra, moved steadily forward towards their objectives. The ground was just a mass of shell holes, with broken wire sticking out here and there. There was not an inch unploughed. Men stumbled to their knees, jumped up and hurried on.

Bad visibility was, at this time, worrying Will a great deal. Dust and smoke were making it impossible to see for any distance. Very early during the advance he lost sight of the battalions both on his left and his right.

"My only hope was to keep close to our own barrage and this principle saved me undoubtedly."

Soon his platoon came up to the curtain of fire which was then ranged on the Hun front line; and their rate of advance from then on was simply regulated by the speed of the barrage. They crossed the enemy front line, Ulrica Trench, without stopping.

They found the German front line trenches had been badly damaged by British shellfire. From a system of defensive earthworks, they had been transformed into a chaotic mass of smashed timber, churned up soil and barbed wire. Such Germans as were left alive had fled to their concrete dugouts.

It was the most gruesome sight Will and his men had ever seen. The German dug-outs had been elaborate constructions extending down to forty feet below the ground. All were now almost completely destroyed, and full of corpses. Hundreds of grey-uniformed figures lay everywhere, most terribly mangled. Some still twitched or kicked, or writhed in agony.

There were limbs, pieces of bodies, and torsos devoid of heads or limbs, or burst open like bags. Entrails and matter, blood and brains splattered the ground. The stink of excrement and quicklime from blown-up trench latrines mingled with the sickly-sweet stench of death.

Following the barrage closely, Second Lieutenant Palstra led Number 14 Platoon deeper into enemy territory. Some twenty yards beyond Ulrica Support Trench ran a ditch. Suddenly a number of long rifle barrels poked out of it and began firing at the approaching platoon. Bullets hissed past the men's ears and pinged off barbed wire.

Will was ready.

"Charge!" he bellowed, running forward, rifle at the ready, his men hot on his heels.

In a frenzy of fury they shouted wordlessly, firing as they ran.

Orders and commands were unnecessary now. The men did their job "as men". Their memory of their comrades left struggling in agony for breath in the gas drenched approach march dispelled any thought of quarter from their minds. Flashes of light stabbed out as the platoon's rifles kept up their rapid fire. The lads blazed away for dear life, firing like machines, fast and methodically.

Men were standing and firing at each other at close range, but the aim seemed to be worse on the German side.

In panic, the Germans jumped out and ran away "like hares", with 14 Platoon shooting at their retreating backs. The fleeing figures toppled into shapeless heaps, all shot down.

At zero hour, the barrage from the German artillery had been falling heavily in front of their own front line. It was a zig-zag barrage and according to Captain Paterson, "the 39th was fortunate enough to get through gaps without many casualties". The British barrage was proving to be extremely accurate. It fell in front of the attacking infantry—a great wall of flame and smoke in the midst of which huge geysers of earth shot skywards. Slowly the wall crept further into enemy territory. For the troops following the dust cloud lit up by the lurid flashes of that barrage, it was almost difficult to realise that danger from the enemy could be present.

Eagerly, 14 Platoon pressed forward behind the line of bursting shells and shrapnel. Too fast. Second Lieutenant Palstra could see that they were in danger of coming under their own shells. "Slow down!" he yelled, his words lost in the thunder.

Deaf to his shouts, half a dozen of his men ran into the fringes of the barrage. He saw one corporal bowled head over heels, rolling in agony and clutching a shattered shoulder. The others stumbled, and collapsed writhing in the grass.

"Stay behind the barrage!" he barked.

Will was left with a mere handful of men. Just then, through the dust haze that made keeping direction and organisation so difficult, he spotted some men of the 39th joining up on his left and two from the Ninth Brigade on his right. They appeared to have no officer.

"We're lost, sir. Can we advance with you?"

"Right you are!" Will replied (or words to that effect), and the men placed themselves under his command.

Leading his motley band, Second Lieutenant Palstra now began to look for landmarks to guide him in the direction of his objective, but in the half light of dawn and with the clouds of dust and smoke caused through the bursting shells, these were obliterated. He simply had to trust to chance and the general direction of the advance. He knew by his watch that the deadline for capturing the final objective was now very close. He had not yet struck the Douve River, nor seen anything else which he could definitely identify as a landmark in this torn-up landscape of mud and barbed wire and shattered tree stumps.

Going by his recollection of the maps he had studied, he decided to bear slightly left, where sooner or later he would strike the Douve, and in the meantime to keep as close to the barrage as possible so as to be able to make the best use of his striking force whenever opposition was encountered. Without hesitation he led his men forward into the thundering, featureless haze.

"I saw nothing to tell me where I was until we ran right on to the wire in front of the stronghold of Grey Farm. I breathed a sigh of relief that I had maintained direction."

Ahead of them, the men could discern the outline of a row of concrete "pill boxes"—hardened blockhouses built to shelter machine gun posts. There were three of them in line, connected with a trench system, and fronted by barbed wire entanglements. On this stronghold British shells were raining down in a manner Will found most comforting.

Approaching closer, he made out the line of the Douve protecting the left, and knew he had reached Grey Farm. His fear that he might have become lost was over.

"I halted them in front of the wire and we knelt down and watched the barrage play on the fortress."

Such was the exhilaration of attack, and probably also such his inexperience that (as he later wrote) he entirely failed to realise the rather awkward position he was in. Ahead of him lay what should be a formidable position, packed with numerous enemy troops, while to his right and left not a sign of anyone—no supporting units at all.

He knew the exact time the barrage would lift from this place. Soon, the British artillery would begin ranging their shells further into enemy territory. When the rain of missiles ceased, the Germans sheltering in that stronghold would, no doubt, open fire.

Will's thoughts raced. Once the barrage lifted there was going to be trouble. What to do? In his mind he argued that unless the attack elsewhere had been a failure, which seemed unlikely, somebody was sure to turn up soon, providing support. If he and his men could capture the pillbox on the left near the Douve, they stood a reasonable chance of holding it until help came. If they stayed where they were, out in the open, they stood more than a reasonable chance of being shot. The last argument was, in itself, sufficiently convincing.

To attack on the flank according to the original plan seemed folly. Their position at the time was in front of the left pillbox. The flank attack would have involved a march across the enemy's front, crossing the Douve in front of the pillbox and recrossing behind the pillbox. In the circumstances the quickest way in was the safest, and the nearest gap between the pillboxes the quickest way in.

Fortunately the wire at this point had been considerably damaged by the bombardment.

4. Mud and Blood

Grey Farm

Imagine Second Lieutenant Palstra shouting "To me, Company!" The small group of dust-smeared Australian soldiers, only a dozen or so, gathers around him, close to the gap. He lifts his voice and says clearly, "As you can probably see for yourselves, the best way in is from the front. We'll take the left pillbox first. Wait for my signal, and then let's give them all their birthdays at once."

"All right, Loot!" the men chorus.

For another minute they all watch the barrage play on the place. Presently the rain of shells begins to move away.

"The moment the barrage lifted," wrote Will, "I was up, and waved the flanks to an encircling attack. Then the Lord smote the Hun before us. For a moment he (the Hun) opened up with his machine guns, then the fools got mad with funk and simply streamed out of the place."

As soon as the attackers entered the enemy wire, panic seized the defenders. They abandoned their guns and dashed away from their trenches in a solid line, some twenty of them. Will and his men planted their feet firmly on the churned-up ground and shot them down. In their savage rage, they felt they were paying back the enemy for their gassed comrades, and for the sinking of the Lusitania, and the execution of Edith Cavell, and all the other crimes they had read about in the newspapers.

"We stood in the wire of Grey Farm and took toll, vengeance for the crimes committed on the land and sea."

Many of the Germans were shot down as they ran, others were killed as they ran into the barrage. Some of the Australians leaped into the trench. They ran along what now proved to be more than a pillbox, and was in fact a concrete redoubt, while the remainder kept firing at any of the enemy who showed themselves.

The fight was over in a very short time.

Second Lieutenant Palstra and his men had successfully captured the enemy stronghold at Grey Farm.

A German concrete gun emplacement, wrecked by British shell fire, at Messines.

AWM E01511

An example of a "pill-box" concrete shelter at Messines (on the right). Will probably took this photo. Typed on a slip of paper glued to the back are the words: "W. Palstra E1295 Huns' walk at Messines, Belgium, in November, 1917. This area was captured by the 39th Battalion during the Battle of Messines, but at the date the photograph was taken it was held by the 14th Brigade. The concrete shelter seen in the right of the picture is a pill-box immediately facing Septieme Barn.

Digging in

As the senior officer in charge, Will's first duty was to ensure there was adequate protection for his able-bodied men. Not until he had taken care of them could he turn his attention to the wounded, including those men of the 39th Battalion who had accidentally run into the barrage and those who had fallen when they attacked the redoubts. Many of the former lay helplessly in shell-holes, where they had managed to crawl for refuge. They lay there bleeding, some groaning piteously, others calling out for help, many ominously silent. Numerous wounded and dead enemy troops also strewed the ground in the vicinity, having been caught by the mine explosions, or the barrage.

It was common knowledge that the German system of defence depended upon powerful early counter-attacks. Now the final objective had been reached, Will knew, his troops should concentrate their efforts upon digging in before the counter-attack came.

The reconstructions of dialogue throughout the following pages are based closely on first-hand accounts.

"We are occupying a former Bosche position," Will told his platoon. "They'll have its range to an inch and can blow us to bits any time they like. We'll dig our own defensive trench line some twenty yards ahead of the captured position."

In fact the men were dog-tired, and Will had to drive them into digging that line, in a forceful manner which would certainly not have been necessary under normal circumstances. He felt for them. They had passed through a most harrowing experience during the approach march, and the subsequent advance had penetrated to a depth of over a mile and a half.

Still, he forced himself to stride up and down the line of the new trench, urging the exhausted men to wield their shovels and entrenching tools and to dig for their lives with phrases like, "Come on boys, put your backs into it! The barrage will lift soon and we'll be sitting ducks if we don't get this trench finished!"

He left Sergeant Barnes in charge of the digging and went to explore the pillboxes forming the German strong-point. Inside, beds were arranged in boarded tiers like bunks in a ship. The floor was littered with empty bottles of wine, beer, soda-water, dirty bedding, empty boxes, ammunition, hand grenades, and other detritus. Pictures of pretty women from 'La Vie Parisienne' magazine adorned the walls.

His exploration of the officers' quarters yielded a case containing bottles of mineral water and a box of excellent cigars. These he carried out and distributed amongst the lads, to help to keep them in good spirits during the tiring work of digging in. Soon he was looking upon the novel sight of men digging under fire with a bottle of "fizz" beside them, while smoking a big German cigar.

Some ten minutes later, on one of these foraging expeditions, Second Lieutenant Palstra learned a lesson. The left redoubt, which was the bigger of the two, consisted of three rooms which he discovered afterwards were connected with a passage. The interior of the whole place was as black as a cave. Assuming that it had been cleared he walked in unarmed, groping with his hands in the darkness, and touched a face. At the same time quavering voices set up a piteous cry of "Kamerad!"[6]

Will's nerves got a nasty jar and he bolted out of that dugout to return with Sergeant Barnes, an electric torch, a Colt, and a Mills bomb. He was astounded to find three Germans, two very much alive and one badly wounded, who looked as if he was dying. Fortunately for Will, all the fight was out of them. Apparently they had been hiding in the passage. They had thrown down their weapons and now stood with their arms raised in the pose of surrender.

Their faces were pale with fear, and they looked distressed to the point of mental breakdown, after what they had been through. Will and his sergeant herded them outside, where he found that a couple more Germans had been discovered alive nearby. He grouped them together and set a corporal to guard them.

By the time the Australian right and left flanks arrived, Will's written report of the capture, together with the four prisoners—the only ones they took—was well on its way to Battalion Headquarters in the breast-pocket of a runner, a man whose role was indicated by the runner's badge, a four-inch-wide red flannel armband.

---

6   It is worth noting that Monash had warned his troops about false German declarations of surrender with the cry of 'Kamerad!' (which translates as 'friend!')

Capt. H. Southby,

7-6-17

39th Battn. A.I.F.

Have taken GREY FARM AAA. Sending 4 prisoners down. Am consolidating position in front of Farm pending instructions AAA

W. Palstra.

2/Lt.

GREY FARM

Time: 4.20 a.m.

More Australian soldiers were arriving at Grey Farm every minute. Some staggered in with bullet or shrapnel wounds. Some had been gassed during the night and were barely able to walk. Others were unhurt, but now that the actual fighting was over everybody seemed to be suffering from a reaction. Second Lieutenant Palstra had to send an N.C.O. to the rear simply because he was too dazed to carry out his job, and the sight of him sitting like a stone image was demoralising.

As for Will, he was the exception. He felt tired but otherwise fine, and fully alert. His mind was fully occupied with coping with the situation, keeping the men cheerful and preparing for the next part of the battle as planned. There was little room for any other emotion.

As soon as possible he despatched a detail to take first aid to the wounded men lying out in the shell holes, and bring in to the shelter of the new trench any who were still able to walk well enough to be supported on the shoulders of their comrades.

Countless corpses lay on the churned-up ground in the vicinity, or half buried in the dirt, arms flung out, faces turned sightless to the skies. Some were missing limbs, or had been blown to pieces, or decapitated. Will told one of his men to search the German dead for items that might prove useful to Army Intelligence.

Light glinted off the waters of the River Douve, some 300 yards away to the north, as it snaked its way through the torn countryside where—incredibly—belts of trees and hedges still stood, though mostly leafless. Will made his way across the broken ground to the left of the redoubts, where the smoky figures of more men in Australian uniforms were trudging towards him out of the thinning dust haze. To his delight he encountered a company of the 39th led by Captain Paterson, D Company's commanding officer.

Imagine the scene. Paterson's tunic, equipment and face are smeared with dirt, sweat and blood. He looks haggard, and weary to the bone. It occurs to Will that he himself must look similar. Nobody has had any sleep for at least twenty-four hours. He snaps a crisp salute, which Paterson returns.

> "Ah, Palstra." A look of relief passes across the captain's face. His voice sounds hoarse—an effect, no doubt, of the gas attack. "Any other officers with you?"
>
> "No sir."
>
> "Then we're the only two in the battalion who have reached Grey Farm."

This meant that Paterson, as the most senior officer still in action, was now commanding the 39th.

> "We have many casualties," Paterson continues. "The battalion is now reduced to less than a hundred men, but as far as I know we are still occupying the full battalion front in the valley."

It was 7.28 am when Captain Paterson sent a message to the commander of the 39th Battalion informing him of their position and strength.

> **"Have only 54 men and 22 N.C.O.s with me and Lieut. W. PALSTRA, on line in front of GREY FARM and joining river DOUVE..."**

The first stage of the Third Division's advance was complete. While the daylight increased and the countryside gradually became visible, the Division's right side settled to the task of fortification, while on the left, the troops waited for the second stage. Close in front of the German second line, the Australians must now bide their time for slightly over an hour while the New Zealand centre worked through Messines.

While waiting for the 34th to take over, the 39th continued "digging in" with very little interference from enemy fire. Having set up their Lewis Gun, they were delving narrow holes into the trench walls into which they could dive if enemy guns opened on them. A party of signallers Paterson had brought with him was excavating a larger hole for their field phone.

As soon as they got it working, the officers could stop sending out runners.

From the sky came the low droning sounds of British aeroplanes. Working in liaison with the artillery, contact patrols were flying low over the forward positions and across enemy lines. Whenever the Germans massed to make a counter attack the British pilots signalled the location of the assembly point back to their own batteries, who promptly concentrated heavy shell fire on it.

Second Lieutenant Palstra could not know it, but by this time, throughout the area behind the Allied lines, there was keen elation at the news that the whole attack was going successfully. The reserve battalions, taking up position on the green slope of Hill 63, enjoyed such a spectacle as they had never known, looking out as it were, from gallery seats upon the Messines Ridge opposite and on the whole scene—the aeroplanes wheeling and fighting in the brilliant sky, the German shells punching roan-coloured dust plumes from the ruins on the summit, lined-out working parties of New Zealanders furiously digging communication trenches up the slope, the Australians preparing for the afternoon attack lining up on their flags, which, like those on a football ground, marked with each battalion's colours the line on which it was to assemble, tanks marshalling in the meadows, batteries of artillery racing up through the long grass, unlimbering, the horse teams trotting back with a jingle of chain, and the gun-crews later opening fire.

Up on the ridge the New Zealanders, who had since 5:30 a.m. been digging the Black Line beyond Messines, had looked out, through the now diminished barrage, over the green Flemish lowlands thickly screened with tree-lined hedgerows, with here and there a sign of some sheltered farmhouse, and, near the horizon, the twin spires of Comines and the more distant steeple of Menin. The scene at the Black Line, as one officer commented, was at this stage "more like a picnic than a battle". The landscape seemed to drowse under a bright sun that promised an exceptionally hot day.

In the course of that summer's morning a few more men re-joined the remnants of the 39th Battalion. They had been wandering around the battlefield, lost, with no landmark to guide them.

Under Fire

Extract from Will's 'War Experiences'—Part 1: Infantry:

> "Later in the morning the position was handed over to the Battalion on the right, and the only remaining Captain in the 39th Battalion took command and moved our force across the Douve."

The sun was high in the sky. Walking back over the shell-torn ground across which the advance had swept, the men of the 39th saw, everywhere, appalling evidence of the efficacy of artillery fire and the stark horror of war. The bodies of their own and enemy dead littered the wrecked countryside, many swollen and already putrefying. Great shell craters yawned in the churned-up fields; unexploded shells, broken equipment and rifles lay about among the debris, splintered tree-stumps reared like strange skeletons here and there, and over all drifted the smoke of battle.

Will climbed a mound of fresh dirt that ranged across the German front-trench line, and found himself on the edge of a smoking crater so wide and deep it seemed impossible that it could have been man-made. It looked more like the gaping maw of an active volcano. The bottom of this terrible pit was littered with a motley detritus of broken timbers, weapons, personal effects and human remains.

As he stepped down he saw Aisbett[7] trudge past, faithfully lugging 14 platoon's heavy Lewis Gun on his shoulder. The battalion had two of the weapons now, because one of the other Lewis Gun sections had managed to hang on to theirs, too.

The 37th Battalion could be seen coming forward in extended order over the rise of Messines Hill. The enemy seemed to be concentrating a great deal of artillery fire in front of the advance, and every now and then the men would drop to the ground as shells burst near them, only to rise and move forward again. Amidst this lethal rain stretcher parties were working across the battlefield picking up the wounded, and enemy prisoners were being escorted to the rear.

Advancing troops had thrown portable wooden bridges across the Douve, though the water was shallow enough that anyone could have waded in and climbed the opposite bank. The 39th crossed the river and hurried across the open ground, with Captain Paterson leading them towards the nearest enemy trench, which was some 300 yards behind the front line.

There they took cover and 'consolidated', occupying the trench in reserve, and supposedly resting, though under such an intense bombardment it was impossible to relax. What's more, the bottom of the trench contained corpses so numerous that the men could not help treading on them. Here and there a dead hand or a blackening head protruded from the earth walls, where a man had been buried—dead or alive—by shellfire.

Towards mid-day the enemy's artillery fire increased and all the German batteries seemed to concentrate their fire along the valley of the Douve and across the top of the ridge. Everywhere, shells were shrieking through the air and crashing into the ground, sending up violent eruptions of mud and scalding blue flame.

---

7   #1208 Aisbett, Harold Edward. Private, aged 19 on enlistment. Trade: Labourer. Single. Address on enlistment: Hamilton, Victoria. "D" Company, 39th Battalion. He was wounded in action several times but returned to Australia in 1919.

Exhausted, the remaining men of the 39th's attack companies crouched in the trench they called "Ulcer Reserve", which had, only a few hours earlier, belonged to the enemy. All about them shells were thundering, a ceaseless stream of flames and whistling roars. Trees of flame arose and blinked out, continuously. The atmosphere thrummed with the whine and hiss of white-hot metal, and the ground trembled, concussion after concussion. Debris and steel fragments pattered down in a never-ending rain.

Suddenly, Captain Paterson fell back, bleeding badly and gasping. He'd been hit. Stretcher bearers carried off the badly injured man to the nearest dressing station.

Extract from Will's "War Experiences—Part 1: Infantry":

"Here in the course of the day we were shelled out of two positions. During the shelling of the first position the Captain . . . was wounded, and I found myself in charge once more, this time with about a hundred men. (This number was increased the following morning when we joined up with the remnants of the other Companies)."

The order to evacuate the shelled-out position was passed from man to man along the trench. Heads down, half crouching, the men of the 39th hurried across the open ground and threw themselves into a section of trench that remained deep and intact.

The enemy artillery did not let up, and it was not long before the battalion received another direct hit, causing numerous casualties. The walls caved in and they were shelled out of their position a second time. Will gave up the idea of occupying captured trenches and got the men out of 'Ulcer Reserve' into shell holes where, on the whole, they suffered fewer casualties.

After such carnage, the battalion was down to thirty-seven "other ranks" and one officer. There, lying prone in the shell-holes, they remained for hours on end under the pitiless heat of the summer sun, listening for the next shell, every nerve screaming in protest against the boundless savagery that they must await, passive and motionless. The tension was intolerable.

Word eventually came back from the dressing station that Captain Paterson had succumbed to loss of blood and the effects of the gas attack. He was too ill to return to duty, so he had handed over the command of the battalion to the highest-ranking officer who was still standing.

Second Lieutenant Palstra was now officially commanding the entire 39th Battalion in action on the front line.

That Long Summer's Day

Second Lieutenant Palstra and the men of the 39th would soon learn, to their elation, that the attack on Messines Ridge had been successful beyond all hopes.

Though powerfully fortified, Messines Ridge from the Douve River to Wytschaete was captured at what the British High Command called "small cost". The cost in Allied casualties was lower than that of any previous battle fought by the British on this scale. When the Allied commanders learned the full details of the battle, they found that the attack had exceeded all expectations. By 1500 hours the entire ridge was securely held, all objectives taken. The front line had moved at last!

On that long summer's day the sun did not set until after 9 pm. Under cover of darkness, Second Lieutenant Palstra sent out men to bring up pack mules with hot food for the 39th Battalion. The stew and tea were barely lukewarm by the time the carrying party had lugged the heavy containers all the way from the cookhouses at the rear to the front line, but the men devoured the food as if famished, finishing the meal with copious amounts of bread and jam.

Soon after the pack mules had been led away with their empty containers, Will's mopping up party returned, reporting that they had found an abandoned trench between Ulna Avenue and Douve Farm. Will thought this position might prove safer than the shell holes, and moved the 39th there after nightfall, in the hope that the enemy might not discover their presence. He would have sent a runner to inform headquarters of the move.

Later on, the battalion's sentries, watching at their posts, reported a large number of men in Australian uniforms approaching. Will was expecting reinforcements, and a wave of relief washed over him as about a hundred of men of the 39th jumped down into the trench. Their leader came straight up to him. His shoulder insignias were the three chevrons and crown of a company sergeant major and Will recognised him as an NCO of 'C' Company.

Imagine:

"Lieutenant Palstra? Company Sergeant Major Lowe reporting sir," says the NCO, saluting smartly. "I've brought reinforcements. Our reserve unit."

"Glad to see you, Lowe," says Will, heartily. "We need every man. We've suffered a great many casualties, besides which, many of our men who became lost during the attack are either still straggling in or have temporarily joined other units.8 We are sparsely spread out along our battalion front. Take your men to reinforce our line in the weakest spot,"—he gives details of the location and allots them a guide—"and assist in digging new trenches."

"Very good sir."

After another salute, the guide leads 'C' Company away along the trench.

The 39th Battalion was defending the front under vile circumstances, commanded by a young ex-office clerk—Will Palstra—who was only a second lieutenant. HQ tried to resolve the leadership issue, but failed.

From Will's diary:

"Two other Officers were sent out to help me, and they were knocked out one after the other.

"Thus for two days and two nights of what General Plumer afterwards described as the heaviest bombardment suffered by any part of the Army, I was in command of the Battalion, cheered the boys, organised the defence, and hung on like grim death under the most awful conditions."

---

8   39th Battalion Diaries: "8 June 1917. Battalion consolidating. Casualties heavy in wounded (killed, light). 14 officers wounded. 285 other ranks. 24 killed other ranks. 145 missing."

Guns pounded all night. Despite the roars and flashes and tremendous concussions, some members of the 39th managed to fall asleep. Exhaustion simply overwhelmed them and they slept where they sat or lay, as if unconscious. Will was aware that sleep would help him function better, so it is easy to imagine that after ensuring that all sentries were at their posts and awake, he crawled into a dugout and snatched a couple of hours of "shut-eye" while overhead and all around, battle raged on.

Thirst plagued Will and his men. The 30th Battalion supplied food and drink, in containers strapped to the backs of mules, which were left, by arrangement, at supply dumps. Under cover of darkness men from the front line were sent across the battlefield to collect them.

These carrying parties endured intolerable conditions. With heavy containers of stew strapped to their backs and their arms full of bags of bread, tins of jam and dixies of tea, the men struggled back to the trench through the darkness. Sometimes the containers leaked along the way. Sometimes they fell into shell holes, or paused, frozen, when an enemy flare lit the landscape with its eerie glare. When the barrage resumed and shells began to rain down around them, they broke into a jog.

When a carrying party returned to the trenches with only one container of tea, Will felt incredulous and annoyed, though he strove not to show it. The parched men needed water even more than they needed food, and tea was all they had to drink However there was nothing to be done except keep calm and carefully dole out the precious liquid, making sure that each man got an equal share, himself included. One container of tea amongst them all was not nearly enough. He sent off a runner with a request for more.

The relief of the 39th

Just before sunrise on 9th June the battalion was relieved by a battalion of the 11th Brigade.

"On the morning of the 9th," wrote Will, "the Battn was relieved and I led the weary remnants of the 39th back to billets. I was just about done myself."

You can imagine the banter the men exchanged as the handover took place; "I hope you left the place nice and clean for us!" "Like a hospital! We're taking most of the chats off to Neep for hot baths."

Weary to the edge of death, half blind with dirt and exhaustion, but exultant at their victory, what was left of the 39th Battalion—one officer (Second Lieutenant Palstra) and 135 men—quietly climbed out of the trenches.

The 39th had been over fifty hours in the attack before it marched back to Nieppe.

In the half-light, shells were falling around them as the men followed Will across the river and struck out towards the Messines Road.

He looked over his shoulder at the tattered remnants of the 39th Battalion tottering behind him, some limping along supported by their mates, some borne on stretchers, others trudging along stoically beneath the weight of their various burdens.

They made it to the road without suffering any casualties. The grimy, unshaven faces of those men as they returned from their first major battle wore a variety of expressions, but whether calm, empty, hollow, carefree, fed-up, jubilant, stoic, happy-go-lucky or expressionless, some common bonds linked them together now, inextricably.

One—the certainty that to wear the 'mud over blood' colour patch was the highest of honours, and their mates of the 39th meant more to them than their own lives.

Two—that they would never be the same.

Three—that they had, at last, been tried, and they had not been found wanting.

The 39th Battalion slogged along with heavy feet and a fog of utter weariness enveloping their minds. Eventually, nonetheless, they found themselves marching into Nieppe.

In that town, hot food was waiting for the exhausted troops, but there were no hot baths available, the closest being at Pont de Nieppe, a mile or two away. Most of the men were guided to comfortable billets where they could rest and make up for the three previous sleepless nights. After the meal Will, though weary to the bone, forced himself to walk all the way to Pont de Nieppe, for he refused to get into a clean bed while covered with the indescribable filth of the battlefield.

Later, scrubbed clean and clad in freshly laundered clothes, he walked back to his billet. There he blissfully sank into a bed with clean sheets, which must have felt like heaven, and instantly succumbed to oblivion.

5. Victory and Glory

Word of the Third Division's success was spreading throughout the AIF. For the veteran divisions, 'Eggs-a-cook divvy' as a term of reproach died with the taking of Messines.

As for Second Lieutenant Palstra, after about eight hours' sleep he walked into the officers' mess that evening and found himself being congratulated by every officer of his acquaintance and more. After the initial surprise wore off, his embarrassment—for he was naturally modest and unassuming—must have mingled with growing self-confidence and a glow of pride.

There was another surprise, too. None other than General Plumer himself, commander of the British Second Army, was in Nieppe overseeing the battle he had so meticulously planned. He was probably in the officer's mess when Will arrived. With his receding chin and bushy, white moustache, Plumer looked like the stereotypical bumbling general. In fact he was quite the opposite—an astute tactician and a meticulous planner who was popular with his men.

"Well done, Palstra," the great man might have said, shaking Will's hand as it had been shaken so often recently. "For two days and two nights of the heaviest bombardment suffered by any part of the Army, you commanded the 39th and hung on with great courage and resourcefulness."

Brigadier McNicholl the commander of the Tenth Brigade was present also, beaming at Will with warm regard. He might have added, "You've made quite a name for yourself, Palstra! You've done us all proud!"

Will recorded in his diary, 'Now I find myself in the somewhat embarrassing position of a hero. I have been congratulated by Gen. Plumer, our own Gen McNicoll, and every Officer who but slightly knows me."

It was a heady feeling. Will had never been drunk, but this feeling was better than inebriation. He must have felt intoxicated by euphoria, by amazement at all that happened, by the flooding joy of being alive, and esteemed, and capable and validated. Not only had he not been found wanting, he had been found excellent.

His courageous, well-judged actions on the battle-field had not only contributed significantly to the establishment of the Australians along the Black Line, but also upheld the honour of the 39th. This was no small feat and, it had been noticed by those in the upper echelons.

The legacy of Magnum Opus

At Messines in Belgium, the marks made on the landscape in June 1917 can be seen to this day. More than a century later, several of the huge craters blown in the earth by the underground mines remain. Some have filled up with rainwater, and reflect the skies like circular mirrors. Some are embroidered with waterlilies. Sheep graze peacefully on the green grass that grows around them, and trees have grown up nearby.

And frighteningly, some of those mines are still waiting to be detonated. 22 tons of high explosive, for example, still lies buried 80 feet below a barn situated next to the farmhouse at La Petite Douve; one of the "lost" mines of Messines.

One of the mine craters, photographed about a century later.
From Wikipedia, "Mines in the Battle of Messines (1917)", titled, "Crater of the 1917 deep mine fired at [an area known as] Caterpillar"

In recognition of valour

On June 11th, after a day spent in billets at Nieppe, the 39th Battalion marched to a camping ground near Kemmel in the vicinity of the village of Neuve Eglise, and Keepaway Farm, where they were to remain for eight days as Corps reserve.

It was at Kemmel that the 39th assembled on the parade ground—shaved, rested, and clad in clean clothes. Music was missing from the parade. The battalion band was not lined up playing its usual stirring tunes. They had been acting as stretcher bearers during the battle, and had suffered casualties. The Band Sergeant and six others were all that was left. Three had been wounded, two rather seriously gassed, and the remaining men were believed to have been slightly gassed on the road up to the trenches and were away in hospital.

It was probably now that Brigadier McNicholl, accompanied by his adjutant and several other members of staff, summoned Captain Paterson, Lieutenant Colonel Henderson and Second Lieutenant Palstra to a meeting in the officers' mess.

Imagine:

There, wreathed in smiles, he tells them all to be at ease, and hands around a box of cigars—which Will politely declines.

"Captain Paterson and Lieutenant Palstra," says McNicholl, "you have both distinguished yourselves these past days. Captain, you captured a strategically important machine gun post at great risk to yourself, showing courage and daring. When the battalion's commanding officers fell, you took charge. The battalion received orders to consolidate on its new position on the north side of the river, and it was there that you were wounded. You remained on duty for several hours after this, but owing to loss of blood and the effects of gas during the approach march you handed over the command to Lieutenant Palstra."

He turns to address Will.

"Earlier in the day, Lieutenant, you were of great assistance to Captain Paterson and throughout the battle you showed much resource and devotion to duty. Though deprived of most of your platoon, you captured the German strong-point at Grey Farm with few casualties, displaying dash and initiative." He pauses, and glances from one man to the other. "Gentlemen, both of you have had the privilege these past days of leading the 39th Battalion and of doing so with flying colours!" Everyone standing around the room is looking pleased and expectant.

"You two fine officers," says the brigadier with a smile, "have both been recommended for one of the Empire's highest honours—the Military Cross."

NOMINATION FOR THE MILITARY CROSS

39th Battalion 2nd Lieutenant William Palstra

On 7th, 8th and 9th June, 1917 at MESSINES for the display of great initiative and ability. This officer was responsible for the capture of an enemy strong point—GREY FARM, and for the consolidation of the BLACK LINE beyond it. He led his men with fine dash, and set a splendid example throughout. His work assisted greatly in the success of the operation. With the exception of the Commanding Officer and the Adjutant of the Battalion he was the only officer left when his Battalion was relieved on the 9th June 1917.

Award for Valour

The story of Second Lieutenant Palstra's exploits at the Battle of Messines was written up, vividly and glowingly, in the Australian newspapers. He was described as "Salvation Army Hero." You can read some of these reports online at "Trove" (trove.nla.gov.au).

As soon as he had the opportunity, Will wrote to his parents. The tone of the letter, dated 12th June 1917, bubbles with optimism.

> Dearest Dad & Mum,
>
> It's all over at last, and I've come through it all OK, and made a wonderful name for myself into the bargain. By now the news of the stupendous battle of X ridge will be well known to you. From my previous letters you will also know that I was in it. Let me chronicle the tale, I marvel at it myself now I can calmly look back on it...
>
> ...I have been recommended for the Military Cross, and am told this distinction will almost certainly be mine...

. . . My nerves seem to be unshakeable, but it has taken me fully three days to get over the overpowering physical weariness caused by those 2 days and three nights of ceaseless activity. I took every step though to get fit immediately. As tired as I was, I went two miles to get a hot bath, and then did about two spells of 8 hrs solid sleeping. Today I am right as rain once more.

I am anxiously waiting for news from Charlie. His Division was in the stunt, although I don't think he was. If I do get the Military Cross will cable you the news straight away. . .

. . . I think the day is measurably nearer when you will have your boys home again. In the meantime remember this, the Hun is beat, and we've got a hand in it.

Love to all,

Will.

Will wrote this exuberant letter while the 39th was stationed at the open-air camping ground near Keepaway Farm. The lingering effects of battle-weariness had almost dissipated and he felt on top of the world. His delight blazed through him like a torch. He had done well. He had made a name for himself.

The war, however, was far from over.

As Will sat in his tent engrossed in composing that letter to his parents, he would have heard repeated explosions from a corner of the encampment field not very far away from the shelters and tents. Allied artillery was firing shells into a nearby town occupied by the enemy.

The 39th's commanding officer Captain Paterson wrote, "The time spent near Keepaway Farm was not a period of undisturbed rest. From a corner of the field, about 500 yards away from the shelters and tents, a heavy howitzer periodically fired shells into the town of Warneton.

"This continued until the third day in camp, when, about midnight on 14th June, the enemy artillery opened searching fire with the evident object of destroying the big gun."

"On this occasion," as Paterson recorded, "the German five point nines[9] did not find their intended target, but found the 39th Battalion instead, causing a rush of half-clad men for the shelter of some nearby trenches."

By good fortune, during the shelling of the 39th by the German howitzers, only one man was slightly wounded.

The explanation of the sudden hail of shell lay in the fact that a German observation balloon had spotted a group of men and vehicles on the Messines Road. Men from the 39th battalion encampment at Keepaway Farm were daily engaged on working parties, repairing this road, which had been badly damaged by shell fire during the battle.

"This work was constantly hampered by the enemy artillery, and there were many narrow escapes. One morning a waggon convoy of the Army Service Corps came trundling along the road, laden with timber, iron and road metal. The 39th working party had commenced to unload the waggons when suddenly a salvo of shells crashed among the men. The drivers whipped their horses into a gallop, the men scattered to find cover, and the road-building material flew in all directions."

After that, the artillery section moved the big gun further away from the camp.

On 24 June, the 39th continued the march to La Douve Valley Camp on the southern side of Mount Kemmel—the highest point on the Flanders Plain.

Here, they passed two and a half weeks in special training, the monotony of which was relieved by athletic competitions and sports of every description. The officers frequently

---

9   The German 15 cm schwere Feldhaubitze 13 (15 cm sFH 13) was a heavy field howitzer. The British referred to these guns and their shells as "Five Point Nines" or "Five-Nines," because the internal diameter of the barrel was 5.9 inches.

arranged cricket matches, into which the men entered with eagerness. These competitions terminated in a Brigade Sports Meeting, in which representatives from each battalion competed, the victory falling to the 40th battalion for military events, and to the 37th for sports.

According to Captain Paterson, "…the value to the men of this period of recreational training was inestimable, and the mental and bodily fatigue caused by the more strenuous days of the preceding month vanished completely."

At Kemmel, the first task was the re-organisation of the thinned ranks of the battalion. The Messines attack had exacted a heavy toll in killed and wounded, and the companies and platoons were greatly reduced in numbers. To fill the vacancies in the commissioned ranks, non-commissioned officers who had shown enterprise and ability during the operations were promoted on the field, so that in the Australian Imperial Force, as in Bonaparte's armies, 'every soldier carried a marshal's baton in his knapsack.'

Life at the front held many a strange contrast. Within three miles of the enemy lines the men could buy, for the trifling sum of six sous, the Paris edition of the London newspapers. They could also visit a cinema theatre in an old barn or abandoned factory, while perhaps not far off, a machine gun fired bursts at an enemy bombing plane. These comforts boosted morale, for they bridged, to a certain extent, the gulf between the horror and hopelessness of war and the cherished things of the outside world which the men had left behind.

Back in Melbourne, in the southern hemisphere, it was winter-time. The streets were ghostly with fog at nights. The tent in which Will's brothers, 21-year-old Frank and 17-year-old Victor had been sleeping in the back garden, was by now threadbare. In places it was torn, and it would have provided scant shelter against a cold Melbourne winter. Fortunately, the boys were now snug indoors, in their own room, because the family had moved to another house.

The parents occupied another bedroom, the girls, 25-year-old Hettie and 19-year-old Blanche, were together in a third bedchamber, and 13-year-old John may have had to sleep in a little bed in his parents' room. The little weatherboard house was filled with the noise and bustle of the large family, who hoped each day that the postman would deliver letters from their two boys at the front, Will and Charlie.

Picture Will's mother Jacoba, a diminutive 58-year-old woman, clad in her black Salvation Army uniform, with her greying hair tied back. She is sitting at a table in a little room just off the kitchen, overflowing with love and concern for her children as she writes a letter, trying to word=paint a comforting picture of their peaceful home.

Letter to Will from his mother:
The Chief Secretary's Office,
Melbourne
161 Westgarth Str., Northcote,
25-6-17 [25th June 1917]

My dear Will,

There was a mail in yesterday, we were wondering if it should have anything for us, seeing we had such a pile last week, but yes, there was one of each of the boys—out of France—the safe passage—the arrival—the base—until going up the line. For a moment I felt as though I must lay my hand on something to keep me steady, but then I thought about the cable we got much later, at any rate you got well through the first month.

I started this letter yesterday, but somehow I could not go on, and today's mail brought us above expectation two letters from you for us, one for Frank and one for Hettie! My word you are in the thick of it my boy, and that straight off after arrival. Strange to say but to hear you talk about it, and describing it, seems to take the first shock away. I belief [sic] I can understand how at last you forget the great danger you are in, and many things included in the day's work are scarcely taken notice of.

The worst is to be thousands of miles away, and always thinking in the other part of the globe.

I am glad we send two parcels away today, one for you and one Charles. Everybody did his share: chocolate—Hettie, figs—John, milk[10] —Vic, cheese—Blanche, butterscotch and something else—Frank, Dad brought some, I knitted the socks. I just mention it, that you may be sure, none of us forgets you.

Now we know that parcels are very welcome, we shall send oftener than once a month. I'll get tomorrow at once the dried fruit and the following mail shall take another. Since April, I have sent three, each with a pair of socks. I thought of sending night socks with the next, it will be September before you receive them. We fill up the corners with lump sugar seeing there is scarcity over there, please do mention everything you want.

Life is moving on in the usual way here, I have been busy today making a nice job of Frank and Vic's room. It has been so foggy lately, and the tent wanted sadly repairing, as it was they could just as well sleep on the lawn, so before the colds [cold weather] got worse, the beds were transferred inside. My word the rooms are bigger than in the other house [at Walker Street], they only fill a corner, leaving a nice square in the midst…

While I am taking about the house, I better tell you where I spend a great deal of the day. The little room next to the kitchen. There is no house on the other corner, so I can see across the paddock over quite a stretch of Westgarth Street and Simpson Street. There is rather a good deal of traffic, so that makes it rather lively.

(Jacoba has drawn a picture of two rooms here)

---

10   Condensed, tinned milk

There it is—x that's where my chair stands. I can keep my eye on the gas stove when any cooking is going on, and sit at the same time in a comfortable cheerful little room, most of my letters are written on that table. Through the kitchen window I can look over the whole garden, with the chickens and ducks in the background. A little bit of difference with the description you gave me where you spend your time—but in this little corner you are never forgotten.

. . . What a change the coming into the war of America has brought about. It is just as though all we thought most important a year ago has gone into the background, and the only question is left—shall democracy win, or the world be crushed under Prussian militarism. It is as though more than ever no young man can keep out of it. I am sure you two boys will do your share to spare the world that calamity.

I have to write Charlie a letter tonight so goodbye for this week my dear Will. God alone can keep you, so I try not to worry, but to trust in Him.

Much love your ever loving,

Mother.

"What a change the coming into the war of America has brought about," wrote Jacoba. The website history.com tells us that, "When World War I broke out across Europe in 1914, President Woodrow Wilson had proclaimed that the United States would remain neutral, and many Americans supported this policy of non-intervention.

"American companies, however, continued to ship food, raw materials and munitions to both the Allies and Central Powers. . . U.S. banks also provided the warring nations with loans, the bulk of which went to the Allies.

". . . public opinion about neutrality started to change after the sinking of the British ocean liner Lusitania by a German U-boat in 1915; almost 2,000 people perished, including 128 Americans. President Wilson demanded that the Germans stop unannounced submarine warfare; however, he didn't believe the U.S. should take military action against Germany. Some Americans disagreed with this non-intervention policy, including former president Theodore Roosevelt, who criticized Wilson and advocated for going to war.

After campaigning on the slogans "He Kept Us Out of War" and "America First," Wilson was elected to a second term in the White House in November 1916. Meanwhile, some Americans joined the fighting in Europe on their own, by enlisting in the French Foreign Legion or the French Air Service, or driving ambulances for the American Field Service.

In response to German U-boat torpedo attacks on merchant and passenger ships, the U.S. severed diplomatic ties with Germany on 3 February, 1916. During February and March, German submarines sank a series of U.S. merchant ships, resulting in multiple casualties.

Finally, on March 1st 1917 the US press reported on a telegram that had been passed to President Wilson the previous day. The British had intercepted and deciphered an encrypted message. This "Zimmerman telegram" proposed an alliance between Germany and Mexico if America joined the war on the side of the Allies. As part of the arrangement, the Germans would support the Mexicans in regaining the territory they'd lost in the Mexican-American War—Texas, New Mexico and Arizona. Additionally, Germany wanted Mexico to help convince Japan to come over to its side in the conflict.

The American public was outraged by this news. Together with Germany's resumption of submarine attacks, it prompted the U.S. to join the Great War. The U.S. officially entered the conflict on April 6, 1917.[11]

The first US troops arrived in France in June 1917. Four months later, on 21 October, the first Americans would enter combat.

---

11   U.S. Entry into World War I. Author: History.com Editors. URL www.history.com/topics/world-war-i/u-s-entry-into-world-war-i-1 Access Date July 30, 2020, Publisher A&E Television Networks. Last Updated July 22, 2020. Original Published Date April 6, 2017 By History.com Editors.

Will's father also wrote to him regularly. In a letter dated 3 July 1917 he asked, "How is the S.A. [Salvation Army] really doing with the military forces, is there anything much in it. . ."

Wiebe would have been pleased to hear confirmation that the Salvation Army was indeed doing a great deal with the military forces. Their services were regularly reported in the War Cry, and though Wiebe might have suspected the reports were overblown, the fighting troops themselves would have vouched for every word.

The Army's little canteens were scattered up and down the Western Front. There, any soldier, regardless of creed or class, could drop in and receive hot coffee and a few biscuits, perhaps a cigarette or two, writing materials and other small but treasured comforts. They could leave letters there, knowing that they would be posted. Enemy prisoners on their way to Prisoner of War cages were given the same hospitality as would be given to a general of the British Army. The soldiers called the Salvation Army "that splendid organisation whose sincerity carries it above and beyond the petty borders of class, creed and country."[12]

British newspapers reported that with anti-German sentiment running high, on 7 July 1917 King George V[13] had changed the family name from Saxe-Coburg-Gotha[14]— popularly known as Brunswick or Hanover—to Windsor. He also relinquished all German titles and family connections.

There were also reports that on 3 July a new poisonous gas had been used by the enemy against British troops at Ypres. It was called mustard gas.

This was a fiendish new gas whose large-scale production had recently been perfected by German scientists. It could be detected by its peculiar garlic-like odour. The effects of mustard gas were particularly cruel. In addition to its lethal qualities, it severely burned every part of the body it touched, scalding the skin, affecting the lungs — if inhaled — and being

---

12   From "Somme Mud"

13   Grandfather of Elizabeth II

14   Gotha aircraft were a series of heavy twin-engine bombers used by the Luftstreitkräfte, the Imperial German Air Service, and the king wished to distance himself from such a name.

especially severe on the eyes.[15] Symptoms rarely showed up immediately, but manifested themselves within twenty-four hours of exposure. Protection against mustard gas was more difficult than against either chlorine or phosgene gas. The body must be completely covered, and respirators must be properly fitted and worn at all times when the merest whiff of gas was suspected.

On 10 July 10 1917 just after dusk, the 39th battalion took over the support trenches near Boyles Farm, west of Messines. The Battalion Headquarters was located in Bristol Castle, a partially demolished brick building which in its more prosperous days had been a civilian post office.

Dark bands of rainclouds loosed deluges upon the battlefields, converting the wilderness of shell craters and churned earth into slippery mud.

During the morning of 16 July the battalion came under heavy enemy shell fire.[16] The bombardment completely demolished many of the dugouts. One of these was being used as the battalion orderly room, and many valuable records were lost. Several men were killed or wounded, and by 11 o'clock the position became untenable, so the battalion moved to the top of Hill 63 where they occupied one of the old trench systems.

Just before dawn on July 18 the 39th again became a target for the German artillery. A prolonged and violent barrage of high explosive shells, accompanied by gas, fell on the battalion trenches for six hours. The was the first time the men of the 39th had experienced 'Mustard Gas'[17] — just two weeks after the enemy had introduced this new chemical weapon. There were fortunately no casualties, the men having observed adequate precautions. The gas lay in trenches and shell holes for several days, and everyone had to be extremely careful when approaching any hollow in the ground. Horses and mules had no protection from the

---

15   Paterson, "The 39th"

16   In his book "Somme Mud", Private Lynch gives vivid descriptions of what it was like to be under shell-fire in the trenches.

17   Mustard Gas – Dichlolthyl sulphide.

gas, and suffered terribly. Shots pierced the air when drivers, taking pity on the creatures, put them out of their misery.

On the night of 20 July, the 39th relieved the 37th Battalion in support trenches atop Messines Ridge and on the outskirts of the ruins of Messines. The trenches were in very bad condition owing to enemy shell fire and the wet weather, and the dugouts in which the men lived were often mere holes, dug in the sides of trenches. Water oozed into them continually, making the interiors muddy and miserable beyond description. It was difficult at the time to obtain timber with which to prop up these makeshift dugouts, and early one morning, owing to the concussion from bursting shells loosening the earth on the surface, most of the dugouts collapsed. Some of the men were buried alive and had to be dug out by their comrades.

Here and there along the trenches, decomposing hands or heads[18] or legs stuck out of the walls. There were grisly sights aplenty, but there were other buried things, too. It was somewhere in the mud of Flanders that Will unearthed a handful of delicate, wafer-thin Roman coins. He stowed them with his most personal possessions, including his diary and letters from home, and looked forward to showing this treasure to his family one day. Some of the new reinforcements trawled the support trenches, gathering such souvenirs as discarded German bayonets, handfuls of shrapnel pellets, the nose caps of shells, flattened German copper-clad machine gun bullets. The old hands knew they would eventually throw them away, rather than be burdened by extra weight.

While occupying this position on Messines Ridge the 39th had to supply numerous working parties, and the fortnight was a strenuous time, full of danger and hardship. German gunners pounded them with artillery fire and it was the rare working party that returned without casualties. Rain pelted down in sheets, and the rough tracks to the front line were in places knee deep in mud which clung to the limbs of any unfortunate man who stumbled.

The 39th would remain in supports until 3 August 1917.

---

18   "On a bend we see a round white object in the trench wall. We go and have a look. It's the top of a man's head jutting out of the wall. The brushing of countless arms against the head has worn the hair and skin off and the bones have become polished like a billiard ball." Somme Mud

During July, enemy gun fire swept unremittingly over the forward and back areas of the British front in Flanders. The enemy, during the weeks succeeding his defeat at Messines, commenced a systematic shelling of Armentières, apparently suspecting that reserves of men would be concealed there for the approaching offensive at Ypres.

The Germans shelled roads, towns and railways continuously, day and night. The Armentières neighbourhood, which had been so quiet a few months previously, became a very active sector of the front. The battalion transport drivers had difficult and perilous duties to perform in taking their limbers up to the front each night along the shell-swept roads approaching the trenches. However heavy the shelling, the limbers always managed to weather the storm and the transport system never once broke down.

Salvoes of high explosive and gas shells rained into the city day and night and many civilians were killed. Others took refuge in the cellars of their houses only to perish from the dreadful effects of poisonous gas, while some were buried under the wreckage of their homes.

Eventually Armentières was reduced to a city of ruins – a place silent and deserted – into which the German batteries still hurled shells in blind fury.[19]

Lewis Gun Course at Le Touquet

The Australian and New Zealand Divisions knew that soon they would be actively involved in the Third Battle of Ypres. They were to take part in three blows to be struck in this operation—The Menin Road, Polygon Wood and Broodseinde Ridge.

The senior ranks had taken note of Will's mettle at the Battle of Messines. Knowing they needed to encourage men with leadership qualities, they decided to boost him along his career path within the army.

Lieutenant Colonel Henderson, the 39th Battalion's commanding officer, summoned Will to his presence. Explaining that the army owed its officers proper instruction and training, he said he was sending Will on a three-week Lewis Gun training course at the

---

19   Paterson, "The 39th"

French seaside village of Le Touquet, beginning on Saturday 28th July. Will was to leave the trenches that very evening. Furthermore, he was to be promoted to the rank of full lieutenant, also on 28th July.

Will must have relished the good news of his promotion. The fact that he was being given the opportunity of the gun course also showed that his superiors had faith in him, and expected him to go far.

"My nerves seem to be unshakeable," he had written, and he was right. How can a man remain as cool and collected as he did, under such extreme pressure, with so many men around him on the verge of emotional collapse?

Did AIF Headquarters perhaps suspect how bad it would be for the 39th in the coming conflict, and did they wish to save Lieutenant Palstra for a possible useful role in the future? The timing of the gun course was certainly fortunate for him.

When Will arrived at the pretty town of Le Touquet, he located his billet and soon settled in to the routine of training. After classes, he and the other officer students probably relaxed by the fire in the common room, playing cards or writing letters or looking out the droplet-spattered windows at the rain-drenched beaches and the grey lines of white- capped waves. Will's thoughts must have strayed to his comrades in the 39th Battalion. They would be defending their lives under appalling conditions in the front-line trenches near Warneton, as the Third Battle of Ypres commenced.

Later, when he re-joined them, he found out exactly how bad it had been.

The 39th defended the front-line trenches throughout this period, holding recently captured ground in front of the town of Warneton. They suffered terrible hardships and horrific casualties. On 5 August the battalion was relieved at last, and the exhausted survivors marched to the little French village of Zoteaux.

It was here at Zoteaux, on Saturday 18th August, that Lieutenant Will Palstra re-joined the 39th after the completion of his Lewis Gun course at Le Touquet. On his arrival, he was briefed on the plans for the forthcoming days.

The Third Battle of Ypres ("Third Ypres") took place on the Western Front from 31 July to 10 November 1917. It was a struggle for control of the ridges south and east of the Belgian city of Ypres in West Flanders, Belgium.

The hour of the 39th Battalion's entry into the Third Battle of Ypres at Broodseinde Ridge was drawing near.

Late on 24th September they received orders to march to the front line the next day. As the men packed their bags and prepared themselves, Lieutenant Will Palstra was summoned to Brigade Headquarters.

Imagine:

> Will enters the room and snaps a well-practised salute.
>
> The Chief of Staff looks up from his desk. "Ah, Palstra!" he says, "You have fresh orders. You've been detailed to act as Brigade Liaison Officer during the forthcoming operation. You will lead a billeting party, travelling ahead of the battalion each day, to organise accommodation along the route."
>
> "Very good, sir."
>
> "You'll have to depart tonight and make all speed to get the job done on time. The men will commence the march first thing in the morning, and they'll need somewhere to stay tomorrow night. I suggest the village of St Pierre."
>
> "Yes, sir."
>
> "It's a fair way off, and all the major roads are heavily congested with traffic. Lorries and wagons crawl along at a snail's pace, marching is far too slow, and since we're not the cavalry, you and your men will use bicycles."
>
> The Chief of Staff hands Will the documents and maps he will require to fulfil his mission.

After leaving Brigade Headquarters Will mustered his billeting party and obtained bicycles for them all. As darkness fell, he set off at the head of the group, pedalling furiously along the uneven cobblestone roads and weaving in and out of the traffic as they headed for the village of St Pierre, some fourteen kilometres away. Their task— to prepare accommodation for the battalion for the first night's halt.

It looked as if Lieutenant Palstra would end up being among the first of the battalion to arrive at the front line.

Will's superior officers clearly thought highly of his navigational skills. In 1916 they had chosen him to lead the 39th Battalion on a route march through Cape Town when the convoy of troop ships stopped there on the voyage from Australia. Furthermore, he had proven his ability to locate Grey Farm through the thick dust haze of the Battle of Messines. Now they trusted him to find his way through a bombed and blasted landscape that was devoid of signs and practically featureless.

"So, from day to day," Will wrote to his parents, "I went forward ahead of the column preparing billets and having a pretty strenuous time, till by and bye the sound of the guns grew louder and soon hostile planes began to drop their nightly souvenirs. Then we got to a small village where we stayed for three days, equipping, patching ourselves up with the various colour patches each of which convey a definite meaning to the soldier.

. . "Tuesday night comes my order to move to forward Brigade H.Q. in the Line as soon as possible."

6. The Menin Gate & Broodseinde Ridge

The Courier-Mail (Brisbane, Qld. : 1933 - 1954)

Wednesday 5 December 1934 p 14

Monash's War Letters,

(Note that the newspaper's editors have provided sub-headings throughout the letter, for easier navigation.)

By the Menin Gate, Ypres,

'October 1, 1917.

'I have just advanced at my addressed battle headquarters for our next stunt, and am writing in a dugout in the eastern ramparts of Ypres, close to the Menin Gate. Until the beginning of the great Flanders offensive in 1917 and even since the close of the second battle of Ypres in 1915, this town has lain under easy reach of the Boche guns, and has been subjected to constant shelling every day and every night.

'Ypres was an old walled town and encircled by ramparts, which presented a sufficient thickness of breast works to be fairly safe against enemy shells. Under, and in the sides of these ramparts, numerous tunnelled dugouts, cabins, and galleries have been constructed during the three years that the British have been defending the town. In one considerable group of such tunnels, just near the Menin Gate. I have established my battle headquarters, for the fourth phase of the battle of Ypres.

'It is in every respect like the underground workings of mines narrow tunnels, broadening out here and there into little chambers, the whole lit by electric light, run by my own portable electric plant. It is cold and dank and overrun by rats and mice, and altogether smelly and disagreeable; but here I shall have to stay for nearly three weeks. Myself, aides-de-camp, staff, clerks, signallers, cooks, batmen, and attached officers are tucked away all over the place, in little cabins, recesses, and dugouts. Our A mess is just like a little cabin of a sailing ship or tramp steamer, and there is scarcely room to move anywhere.'

'This Was Ypres'

'The town of Ypres, once a marvel of mediaeval architectural beauty, lies all around us a stark, pitiable ruin. For three years it has been dying a lingering death, and now there is nothing left of its fine streets, its great square, its cathedral, the historic Cloth Hall, its avenues and boulevards of fine mansions, its hospitals, its town hall or its straggling suburbs but a charred collection of pitiable ruins, a scene of utter collapse and desolation.

'Although we have pushed back the Boche several miles east of Ypres and most of his guns and Howitzers are now beyond range, yet he still shells the town intermittently with long range high velocity guns, and every day a few more of the gaunt spectral pillars which once were fine historic buildings are toppled over and crumbled into dust. There can be little doubt that it cost the enemy, in actual ammunition, many times more to destroy the town than ever it cost to build it.

'Difficult as it is to convey any idea of the destruction of Ypres, it is simply impossible to describe the life and turmoil in the whole area, from Poperinghe forward through Vlamertinghe (also destroyed) and Ypres. as far as our present forward position. It is one enormous medley of military activity of every conceivable description, and the traffic on the main roads is simply incredible. Imagine the traffic in Elizabeth Street [Melbourne] for an hour after the last race on Cup Day multiplied tenfold and extending in a continuous line from Flemington to Sandringham, and streams of men, vehicles, motor lorries, horses, mules, and motors of every description moving ponderously forward at a snail's pace in both directions hour after hour, all day and all night, day after day, week after week, in a never halting, never ending stream.'

'Through Mud to Victory'

'Yet in this apparent confusion and turmoil are order and system, and every vehicle has a definite starting point, destination and purpose. If you could stand for half an hour at what we know as the Asylum corner, at the southern entrance to Ypres, where the roads from Dickebusch and Poperinghe meet, you would see this never-ending stream ploughing its way slowly and pain fully through the mud, man and horse plastered to the eyes in mud, and a reek of petrol and smoke everywhere.

'Here comes a body of fighting troops, tin-hatted and fully equipped, marching in file into the battle area, to carry out a relief of some front-line unit; there follows a string of perhaps 100 heavy motor lorries, all fully loaded with supplies; a limousine motor car with some divisional staff officer, a string of regimental horse and mule-drawn vehicles

> going up to a forward transport park, some motor ambulance waggons, more heavy motor lorries. A long string of remount horses, marching in twos, is seen going up to replenish wastage, a great 12-inch howitzer, dragged by two steam traction engines, returning from the workshops after repair of injuries received, more infantry, thousands of them, more ambulances, more motor lorries, a long stream of Chinese coolies, smart and magnificent of stature, more lorries, every now and then a staff motor car struggling through the melee, dozens of despatch riders on motor bikes threading their way skilfully between the gaps, a battery of artillery all fully horsed and clattering and jingling, motor lorries again, heavily loaded with artillery ammunition, a motor car, a string of motor waggons bringing forward broken stone and road-making materials. And yet all this conveys no real ideal of the real thing. There has been said no truer thing than that war is work.'

On the evening of 2 October, Lieutenant Palstra received orders to proceed immediately to 10th Brigade's Battle Headquarters in the Line, which was situated in the once-great Belgian city of Ypres. He lost no time in hitching a ride on one of the many lorries heading in the direction of that city.

"Within an hour I am on my way. Caught a motor lorry along the Poperinghe-Ypres road up to the Menin gate Ypres."

The booming of the guns resounded on every ridge, the flare and flame of battle rose and fell on the horizon. All through the night a stream of men, horses and guns pounded over the cobbles of the battered road to Ypres. Will's lorry bumped along in the stream of traffic.

At length the vehicle stopped. You can imagine the driver, probably a British soldier, saying, "'Ere we are, sir. The Menin Gate. That's far as I go in this direction."

Will thanked him for the lift, jumped out, and pushed the door shut. The truck pulled away and Will was left at the roadside staring at the blasted ruins of the famous Menin Gate, once the imposing entrance to the city of Ypres.

The Menin Gate occupied the eastern wall of the city. It became known as the Menenpoort, or Menin Gate in English, because the main road leading out through, after crossing a bridge spanning the city moat, led onwards to the small town of Menen.

The gateway had begun its existence in medieval times, as a simple, narrow portal in the walls of the fortified settlement. Major works during the 17th century had turned the Gate into a magnificent, towering structure. Its deep central arch, well over 100 feet high, was flanked by two lesser portals, all topped with ornate entablatures and carved stone panels.

THE MENIN GATE BEFORE THE WAR, CIRCA 1912 (SOURCE UNKNOWN)

During the First World War, countless British and Commonwealth soldiers passed through the Menin Gate on their way to the front lines. Some 300,000 of them were killed in the Ypres Salient. 90,000 of these soldiers have no known graves.

During his youth in Belgium, Will had witnessed that Gate standing whole and proud and magnificent beneath the sky. By the time he reached it in 1917, the old structure lay crumbled in ruins, its carved limestone lions badly damaged by shellfire. Yet that was as nothing compared to the devastation that reigned in the city beyond. Every building in that once-thriving metropolis had been bombed beyond recognition.

Ypres had paid a heavy price for being situated in a strategic position. It was at the centre of a network of roads, and stood in the path of Germany's planned sweep across Belgium.

"The town of Ypres," wrote Monash, "once a marvel of mediaeval architectural beauty, lies all around us a stark, pitiable ruin."

In October 1917 Will passed through the Gate and entered the desolation of Ypres. The dim, rubble-strewn streets, crowded with vehicles, were illumined by the erratic flashes of artillery and rockets.

"Ypres itself," he wrote later, "is a grand monument of the desolation of war. Not one stone in this once large and prosperous city is undamaged or in its place. The streets are tracks among huge mounds of brick dust."

As a child in Belgium Will, with his family, had visited the Flemish city's famous 13th century Cloth Hall. He recalled it as a beautiful, stately building.

"I saw the remains of the Cloth Hall shattered beyond hope of repair," Will wrote. "It's a tragedy almost as great as that of the dead-strewn battle field."

Even among the ruins, people had to earn a living. A bedraggled French street-vendor approached Will, carrying a tray of souvenirs. The pressed metal badges were small and light enough not to weigh down his luggage on the way home. Having selected one depicting two horse-drawn wagons loaded with goods and the word YPRES, Will paid the man with a coin.

This badge would remain among the family treasures for more than a century.

The Battle of Broodseinde Ridge

The battle of Broodseinde Ridge was the third operation launched by General Plumer as part of the Ypres offensive of 1917. The 39th's approach-march to the trenches fronting the ridge took place on 3 October. It was Lieutenant Palstra who guided the entire battalion to the jumping-off place for the assault.

Ominously, the weather was changing. Clouds massed in the night skies, blotting out the stars. The first rumbles of an approaching thunderstorm sounded above the boom of guns, the roar of enemy aeroplanes and the crash of bombs bursting.

The attack began before dawn on 4 October 1917. The Australian troops were shelled heavily on their start line, and a seventh of their number were killed or injured even before the assault began. When it did, the attacking troops were confronted by a line of enemy infantry advancing towards them; the Germans had chosen the same morning to launch an attack of their own.

Will's role was that of a messenger, travelling back and forth amidst the fighting. He carried reports from the 39th battalion to Brigade HQ, whereupon the Brigadier sent a runner back to Divisional HQ with Will's notes and maps. Will also acted as a guide for burial parties.

"Another of my jobs was to collect stretchers and spades with a party and take them up, all the time with the beastly Hun shells and machine gun bullets cutting up the ground all over the place.

"I had the inevitable number of exciting moments, especially once on a skyline when the Hun opened up on me with a machine gun, and lead whistled and hummed round about for a couple of minutes."

Will later wrote in his memoirs,

> "Prisoners streamed in by hundreds. It was a record bag. They surrendered in parties of 30 and 40, officers and all. They were Guards and Hanovarians, most of them quite a good type, but morale completely gone. We put them on to carrying stretchers through the boggy ground.
>
> "Each batch of prisoners was viewed greedily from afar off and as soon as they got near our lads the astonished Hun found about half a dozen hands in his pockets looking for souvenirs.

"The scenes on a battlefield are fearful though, too horrible to describe.

There were dead unburied as far back I should say as the battle of the 31st July."

The Australians forged on through the German assault waves and gained all their objectives along the ridge. It was not without cost, however, and the Australian divisions suffered 6,500 casualties.

The Allies, nevertheless, considered Broodseinde a great triumph. Now it was time for the battalion, worn out and battered, to re-organise itself, in readiness for the assault on Passchendaele Ridge.

> Oct 7th 1917 O.A.S.
>
> "Dearest Mother & Dad,
>
> "The night before last I came out of what the papers this morning are calling the biggest British victory of the war, namely the battle of the 4th—5th October on an eight mile front East and North of Ypres. I did not expect to be in it, as a matter of fact I had been detailed by Battn to remain behind. However Brigade collared me as Liaison Officer, and so I was actually the first of our Battn. in the Line…
>
> 8/10/17
>
> Today is my birthday. Nobody here knows the fact so am spending it quietly, and my thoughts are frequently with you. God willing the next will be at home.
>
> Love to all from
>
> Will

7. Passchendaele

"Third Ypres" lasted for more than three months, and incorporated a series of shorter battles such as the Battle of the Menin Road, the Battle of Polygon Wood, the Battle of Broodseinde, the First Battle of Passchendaele and the culminating attack, the Second Battle of Passchendaele, between 26 October and 10 November 1917.

The men of the 39th could not know that the experience for which they were preparing would become infamous in the annals of mankind. Thereafter the Third Battle of Ypres, including the assault on Broodseinde, would afterwards be called by the name of the village that had become the last objective—"Passchendaele".

History remembers the name of that small Belgian village as synonymous with the Great War's most horrific bloodbath, and symbolic of the madness and senseless carnage of the Western Front. "Passchendaele" was to become a "symbol of the mud, madness, and senseless slaughter of the Western Front."[20]

---

20   Encyclopedia Britannica: Battle of Passchendaele World War I [1917] By R.H. Roy.

In Australia, as in many other countries, numerous towns and streets across the land have been commemoratively named after First World War battles. Passchendaele is one such name; it appears repeatedly.

In his "Memoirs" of 1938, Lloyd George wrote, "Passchendaele was indeed one of the greatest disasters of the war . . . No soldier of any intelligence now defends this senseless campaign …"[21]

The 39th Battalion, which had started the day with just over 1000 men, lost 210 in one morning, with hundreds wounded.

The attacks of Third Ypres, which continued into November, petered out in this rain and mud.

Extract from Will's 'War Experiences' — Part 1: Infantry.

"The percentage of killed to wounded was much greater at Passchendaele compared with Messines. Much equipment was also lost. . . The whole Division had in the course of a couple of weeks reached a stage where it required a thorough rest and re-equipping. My own Brigade was embussed behind Ypres and taken to Zoteux, a village some twelve miles south-east of Boulogne."

In the last weeks of October Will received a letter from his Anzac brother Charles, now a full lieutenant, who had been hospitalised with fever. Will immediately sent his parents a cablegram reassuring them that both their soldier sons were still alive, and "both-safe-end-November"—meaning that neither would be back on the front line until at least the end of November. Hearing from Charlie was a glimmer of light at a dark time.

At this bleak hour Lieutenant Palstra's life was, however, about to take another unexpected turn.

---

21   "War Memoirs of David Lloyd George" by David Lloyd George. Ivor Nicholson & Watson Ltd. (January 1, 1938)

"The attack towards Passchendaele ridge was my last infantry battle... A few days after arrival [at Zoteaux], I left the Battalion, having received word that my longstanding request for transfer to the Australian Flying Corps had been granted."[22]

Lieutenant Palstra was to leave the infantry and become a pilot.

The 39th Battalion

This is where we leave behind that valiant band of comrades who made up the 39th Battalion, whose mascot was a bulldog, who sang songs in the streets of Ballarat in 1916, and who fought and died on the Western Front.

No doubt it was a bittersweet parting. Will's comrades would have wished him well, while perhaps envying him his good fortune. The bonds formed in a battalion of fighting men are strong indeed, and there would have been many promises of future meetings made, "See you after the war, you lucky devil!"

---

22   Extracts from Will's 'War Experiences' - Part 1: Infantry:

Part II: 1917-1918

Wings and Kings

The Australian Flying Corps had finally accepted Will's application to become a pilot!

It would have been with immense joy that he received this unlooked-for news. After waiting so long without hearing anything from the AFC, perhaps he had given up hope. His acceptance letter was a ticket to a new life—a life in the clouds, away from the mud-slathered trenches; a life of adventure, excitement, and enormous prestige, not to mention higher pay!

Aviation 1912 to 1916: The militarization of aeroplanes

By the end of October 1917, when Will left the 39th Battalion and departed from the Western Front, aeroplanes had not been around for very long. Indeed, the first manned, powered, heavier-than-air flight had taken place in France in 1890, only a year before he was born.

At the outbreak of the Great War, there had been no such thing as an aeroplane that was capable of combat. Flying machines were still seen as a sportsman's plaything, with little practical application. Most military authorities had not yet realised their full potential as war machines. Both the Central Powers and the Entente Powers found them useful for reconnaissance—that is, for flying across the enemy's lines and finding out what he was up to. Apart from that, the only use for aeroplanes was to enable the pilot or his passenger to try to shoot the enemy with a rifle, or drop a few bombs over the side.

There was no known effective way to arm aircraft. Furthermore, aeroplanes could not transport more than one or two people at a time, they were terribly flimsy, and they couldn't carry more than a light load.

The materials for building larger, stronger aircraft simply did not yet exist. Due to availability, low weight, and the prior manufacturing experience of the builders, most early aircraft were made of wood, braced with wires and struts and covered with fabrics such as cotton and canvas. Prior to around 1920 most aeroplanes had two sets of wings (which is why they were called biplanes) because this design imparted strength to the fragile wooden flying machines. Piloting them was a highly dangerous occupation; often they would just spin out of control and crash, killing the crew.

In his book "Early Birds", H. C. Miller tells us that during the first few weeks of war in the air, "Enemy pilots flying past each other on observation missions merely cast perfunctory glances at one another, although some ill-mannered fellows were so rude as to make threatening gestures. Eventually pilots on both sides began the habit of stashing two halfbricks in their flight jackets prior to takeoff, for the purpose of hurling them at the nearest enemy airman's head. More ingenious dirty tricks followed, including dropping chain links on the engine cowling of a foe's plane in the hope that it would snag his propeller and force it to stop.

"In the latter part of 1914, German and Allied war-planes carried cardboard boxes full of flechettes—steel darts with razor-sharp fins. Dumped on an enemy plane's wings, they were certain to rip them to shreds. They were equally certain, when aimed at the ground, to wreak havoc among those enemy soldiers in the vicinity of where they fell.

"Some pilots, in their desperation to 'get things moving', resorted to firing pistols, rifles, even shotguns at whatever enemy planes came within their line of sight, an act of aggression far more symbolic than effective."[23]

Before 1915 the aeroplane was not considered to be a fighting machine, because if planes were ever to be really useful in that respect, they would have to be armed with machine guns. For a pilot to be shooting and flying at the same time was too difficult. Clearly the best advantage was to be gained by mounting a machine gun above the engine cowling, right behind the propeller, so that pilots could point their machines at the enemy and just begin firing. There was one problem, however; by doing so, the pilot would simply shoot his own propeller to pieces.

In August 1915 the new German warplane, the Fokker E.I, with synchronization gear, entered service. A gun synchronizer was mounted on the front of the aeroplane, allowing the on-board gunner to shoot machine gun bullets through the rapidly spinning propeller without damaging the blades. This fixed armament was directed by aiming the aircraft, rather than the gun, at the target. By April of the following year the British had developed their own synchronization gear.

"The importance of the synchronised machine gun for air warfare cannot be overemphasised," wrote HC Miller.

Heavier and faster fighter planes armed with synchronized machine guns began rolling off the Royal Aircraft Factory's assembly line at a rapid rate. The airmen invented a tactic called 'ground strafing'. Squadrons of planes would dive out of the clouds, firing away for all they were worth, mowing down the enemy before they had a chance to take cover.

---

[23]   Early Birds: Magnificent men of Australian aviation between the wars." H.C. Miller

Says Miller, "By the spring of 1916 French Spads, English Sopwiths and German Albatrosses, armed with double machine guns of unprecedented firepower, were raising havoc with ground strafing."[24]

Accelerated by the exigencies of war new tactics were developing all the time, new specialised aircraft were being manufactured, and people finally realised that the aeroplane had a military future.

Aviation captured people's imagination like nothing else. In "A Passion for Wings", R. Wohl writes, "Flight was seen as something spiritual and moving, as well as being aesthetically pleasing. The early aeroplanes were considered things of beauty."[25]

Aeroplane pilots, swooping about in the clouds, were viewed as brave 'knights of the skies', and some people, even enthusiastically compared them to angels. The term 'ace' was coined for an airman who had shot down five or more enemy planes.

Lieutenant Palstra had distinguished himself on the field of battle. His courage had brought him to the attention of his superiors. Perhaps someone at HQ decided to look into his files, or perhaps he himself now mentioned to someone in the upper echelons that he had, back in 1916 on Salisbury Plain, applied to join the Royal Flying Corps. Since that date, the world of aviation had changed.

Excerpts from Will's Diary:
> Friday Oct 26th Zoteux—Pas de Calais. Received wire informing me I am selected for training A.F.C. (Australian Flying Corps) and to proceed to England at once.

After waiting so long without hearing anything about his application to become a pilot, Will must almost have given up hope. His acceptance letter was a ticket to a new life—a

---

24 ibid.

25 A Passion for Wings—Aviation and the Western Imagination 1908-1918. R. Wohl. Yale University Press, 1994.

life in the clouds, away from the mud-slathered trenches; a life of adventure, excitement and prestige, not to mention higher pay! Life seemed filled with promise.

The Australian Flying Corps (AFC) was at this time a branch of the Australian army. In 1916 no independent air forces existed anywhere in the world, aviation being a branch of the army and the navy. The RFC was the British unit. In 1918 the RFC would become the Royal Air Force, the world's oldest independent air force.

Since its inception in October 1912 the AFC had flourished and expanded rapidly. It now comprised four squadrons. It was destined to become the RAAF in 1921—the second-oldest independent air force in the world.

That time, however, was still far off.

A fortnight's leave in Scotland

By Thursday November 1st Will had reported to Arkwright Rd., Hampstead, where he was examined by R.F.C. (Royal Flying Corps) Standing Medical Board No. 9. He was in such bad shape after his experiences at Passchendaele that he was classed as 'temporarily unfit' and given 14 days leave.

It's not unlikely that Will was suffering from extreme exhaustion and debilitation after having fought in three horrific battles and endured, for weeks, the terrible conditions of the trenches. He was also ill with influenza during part of that fortnight. The "Spanish Flu" did not take hold globally until January 1918, but Will was one of its early victims.

He went to stay with a family called the Taylors (possible Salvation Army people), in Glasgow, Scotland. What a welcome relief those fourteen days of leave must have been. In the home of these friends he could bathe and relax and eat home-cooked meals, and sleep between clean, lice-free sheets in peace, with no shells exploding nearby and no bugle calls to rouse him to battle.

Flying Machines

The Australian Flying Corps

The AFC was at this time a branch of the Australian army.[26] In 1916 no independent air forces existed in the world, aviation being a branch of the army and the navy. The RFC (see endnotes) was the British unit, the "Aviation Section, Signal Corps" was the designation for US squadrons, the French had the *Aéronautique Militaire* and the German Army Air Service had "*Die Fliegertruppen des deutschen Kaiserreiches*", most often shortened to "*Fliegertruppe*". It was renamed *Luftstreitkräfte* on 8 October 1916 and later became the *Luftwaffe*.

From "Reckless Fellows: The Gentlemen of the Royal Flying Corps" by Edward Bujak:

> "The two largest pools of Empire pilots were from Canada and Australia.
> Unlike Canada, Australia formed its own operational Flying Corps with four squadrons flying alongside the RAF in 1918."

---

26   It was not until 1 April 1918 that the RAF, the world's first independent air force, would be founded by amalgamation of the British Army's Royal Flying Corps and the Royal Naval Air Service. The Royal Australian Air Force, the world's second oldest independent air force, would be formed on 31 March 1921.

How were prospective pilots chosen? An Australian War Memorial article entitled "Those Who Would be Airmen"[27] states: "Not everyone was suited to this new field of military operations. Light horsemen or "bushmen" were thought to be physically fitter and have quicker reflexes and a better "character" than other men; they were common in No. 1 Squadron. Many of its later recruits came from the ranks of the Light Horse; most of these already had years of active service. The Squadron also drew men from other backgrounds: the AFC's only Victoria Cross winner, Captain Frank McNamara, had been a schoolteacher.

"Many of those who joined the squadrons on the Western Front also had prior service. The list of candidates for appointment to become flying officers in June 1918, for example, records a mixture of officers and other ranks: some had been gunners, others clerks, drivers, infantrymen, or members of the medical services. One man, a veteran of Gallipoli and the Western Front, had found his way into the 4th Australian Sanitary Section before being accepted into the AFC. Many were recommended for admission by their commanding officers on no other ground than their good record as soldiers in the line.

"Given the nature of warfare on the Western Front, it is not difficult to imagine why men would seek to transfer into the AFC. Many had experienced the misery and squalor of the trenches. Those who knew they would face danger as long as they were in the AIF, preferred to face it in a corps which offered the promise of independence and glamour, as well as a degree of comfort unknown to the men in the trenches. Those who served in the Middle East, although spared the worst miseries of the Western Front, shared a similar desire to escape their own discomforts: sand, dust, and flies. Men who had already served in the ground forces reasoned that if they survived the day's flying, they would at least have the chance to sleep in a comfortable bed.

"Not everyone, however, survived the day's flying. Many pilots were killed in accidents long before they could join a line squadron. Over a third of the AFC's wartime fatalities occurred in Britain."[28]

---

27   www.awm.gov.au/atwar/ww1_flying.asp

28   Those Who Would be Airmen. Australian War Memorial.

When Will's leave was over, he spent a fortnight at the Australian Flying Corps Details Camp in Wendover. From there he was sent to No 1 School of Military Aeronautics in the town of Reading; Having arrived on Friday 7th December 1917, he was enrolled in Course 44, Class 9 and was billeted at Wantage Hall, University College.

For the duration of his stay at Reading, Will would not so much as set foot in an operational flying machine. That would come later when, following their period of theoretical learning at Reading, cadets would be posted to a Training Squadron in the UK.

"The 'No 1 School of Military Aeronautics' provided preliminary training for cadets and taught theoretical aspects of flight; including map reading, gunnery and mechanics. A small airfield was established at nearby Coley Park in around 1917."[29]

"Many of the instructors were veterans of the Western Front. Still young men, they often struggled to teach the cadets who were of a similar age." [30]

Will took to aviation theory like a duck to water, and was good at it. As he later wrote to his mother,

> "Scored terrifically the other day by giving proof of a certain aerodynamical technicality which baffled a Class and its instructor for fully 5 mins."

In a letter to Will dated 13 December 1917 his mother Jacoba wrote,

> Now your second letter . . . the Flying Corps. It was last Tuesday that I came to Dad's office and found it there. I must confess it nearly took away my breath. All the danger and anxiety it would bring me in future came as an avalanche over me. Well! that boy, why must he pick out the most dangerous thing.

---

29   Ashworth, Chris (1990). Action Stations: Military airfields of the Central South and South-East. Patrick Stephens Ltd pg. 245

30   Hart, Peter (2 October 2008). Aces Falling: War Above the Trenches, 1918. Hachette UK.

Then your letter (26.10) to me last night, and after having gone through it once—twice—I could not say anything, or rather would not, that would cause you to regret your step. Of course, I shall shiver all over me, and feel my heart sink into my boots, when I shall think, or may be, see you, hovering high up into the air—but—the very idea what it means to you as explained in your letter, makes me say I would not lay a straw in your way, not even if it only caused to make you feel less happy over it. I am too pleased that you feel that at last you shall get into work for which you have been longing for years. I am afraid that the blood of two sailor grandparents is after all in your veins.[31]

The last I have to say is—I will not accept your invitation to go in your bus [aircraft], unless in time I change my mind, till up now I must have something solid under my feet. But besides all this, it is a great honour for you to be placed in the [Air] Corps in this way, without having had any training in that direction before-hand. How did you manage it? It will be awfully interesting to hear how you are getting on.

As one is used in wartime to live by the day, I cannot deny, that the prospect of you being for months in England for training, is very comforting to me. What a style it will be, what with the white wings [insignia on his uniform] and what with the Military Cross, Vic [Will's younger brother] will go clean off his head when he sees you...

---

31   Jacoba's father and Wiebe's father had both been sea captains. The sea was the closest metaphor for the air. Even the terms 'airship' 'pilot' etc. were derived from seafaring.

The Military Cross

And what of the esteemed medal to which Jacoba had referred? On 12 December 1917, the day before she sat down to write that letter, Will was at Buckingham Palace. None other than King George V, grandson of Queen Victoria and grandfather of Queen Elizabeth II, personally invested him with the Military Cross.

The official description of the actions that earned Will the Military Cross:

> "HIS MAJESTY THE KING has been graciously pleased to confer the Military Cross on the undermentioned officer, in recognition of his gallantry and devotion to duty in the Field:
>
> "Second Lieutenant WILLIAM PALSTRA, 39th Bn.
>
> "For conspicuous gallantry and devotion to duty. He led his men with the greatest dash to the capture of an enemy strong point, setting a splendid example throughout. With the exception of the Commanding Officer and the Adjutant of his battalion he was the only officer left when they were finally relieved."

Four days later Will gleefully wrote the following words to his parents, on the letterhead of the Australian Flying Corps:

To return to Wednesday. I presented myself outside Buckingham Palace at 9.45 am, and was ushered into one of the many beautiful rooms in this royal edifice. I believe it was the Queen Victoria Room.

At about 11 am, quite a considerable band of quondam heroes having gathered, in came one of the spare Generals who seem always to be floating around here looking for a job. Our catechism was brief, consisting of a few simple instructions as to rules of procedure in the Royal presence. At last the name of one W.P. M.C. was called and entering a room of Regal but very tasteful and simple pretensions the following met his gaze. On the left His Majesty dressed in the Uniform of a Field Marshall of the British Army, and standing in front of a gold chair. Opposite H.M. and at the other end of the room, a Guard of Honour composed of Indian Officers, spare Generals here and there standing like new subs on parade and seemingly trying to do their best to look as much like the furniture and general landscape as possible.

In walks his nibs W.P. aforementioned, bows according to instructions and then walks up to H.M. and stands to attention.

A spare General makes himself generally useful by running up with a little silver cross looking very magnificent against the background of a royal purple cushion on which it reclines.

H.M. takes said resplendent decoration and pins it above the left tunic pocket of one W.P. and expresses his pleasure at being able to do so. Asks him what he is doing now, and appears quite interested to know he is training at Reading for the Aust. Flying Corps. Shakes hands with one W.P. very cordially. One W.P. steps back, makes another graceful(?) bow and retires through another door literally covered with glory. Outside the crowd cheer the hero who retires very modestly at accelerated velocity.

The laughable part is that now I have got my much coveted decoration I don't in a way know what to do with it. I can't carry it about with me everywhere, and I am almost afraid to send it home lest some U beast should "hate" it[32]. I think the upshot will be that I will risk it and send it on to you.

A SOLDIER (NOT WILL) RECEIVING A MEDAL FROM THE KING. SOURCE: HISTORYPLACE.COM

Will commenced Christmas leave on Sunday 23rd December and went to stay with a family in Sussex over the Christmas holidays.

---

32   'U-beast'—U-boat. 'Hate"—enemy fire.

The winter of 1917 was very cold. I like to think that Will enjoyed all the festive trimmings of Christmas that wartime shortages would allow, including roaring fires.

Somehow, through sheer luck, he had been spared two Christmases in the trenches, facing the horrors and perils of the front line.

The rest of the 39th Battalion was not so fortunate.

So ended the year 1917. Will was glowing with pride in his achievements, and fired up by the prospect of a future filled with excitement and glory. Charlie, too, was safe for the time being, and letters from the family back in Australia assured him that all was well with his loved ones.

On 30 December 1917 in London, Big Ben remained silent at the stroke of midnight. The bells of its famous tower had stopped ringing during the Great War, so 1918 commenced quietly, in darkness.

What would the new year bring?

1918: Flying School

Jan 1st, 1918 found Lieutenant William Palstra studying the theory of aviation at Wantage Hall, Reading, England. On Saturday Jan 26th he sat for his final exam in Aerial Navigation. The following Monday he drew his flying kit—his AFC pilot's uniform—from stores, and spent the day in London.

Flying could be a dangerously cold business. Temperatures plummeted at higher altitudes, and planes were unheated and unpressurized.

By 1917, First World War aviators generally wore a suit called the "Sidcot", an outfit that was better at keeping out cold air than the earlier flight suits, which consisted of anything that could keep a man warm, including knitted woollen mittens, sweaters and mufflers.

Aviators' breeches resembled jodhpurs, being flared above the knee to permit climbing into open cockpit aeroplanes. Leather riding boots clad the feet, while goggles and face masks protected the face from frostbite. Will mentions that he had a leather flying-cap.

Will wrote (with his usual brevity) in his diary on Tuesday 29th January,

"Travel from Reading to No 5 Training Squadron A.F.C. under Major Petre D.S.O.[33] M.C. SHAWBURY SALOP."[34]

No 5 Squadron had been formed at Shawbury in England on 1 September 1917 and provided training to the Australian Flying Corps in Britain during the Great War. After completing their training, Australian pilots would be posted to the operational squadrons based in France.

Will was fortunate to be at flying school at this period of the war, rather than earlier.

The delay in his acceptance into the AFC had worked in his favour.

In 1917, the RFC had introduced the improved "Smith-Barry" system of training. This halved the high fatality rate of trainee pilots. Prior to this, cadets would receive lessons from an instructor who was usually a pilot from an operational squadron on the Western Front, sent back to take a break from fighting. These pilots had never been taught how to instruct, since there were no training schools for pilot instructors.

The new system was better, nonetheless fatal accidents during flying training were still frequent. The hard part about flying was surviving long enough to get to the front line. A great many men were "napooed" in training accidents long before they even reached a line squadron.[35] Flying a war-plane—or any aeroplane, during those early days—was a dangerous vocation.

---

33   Distinguished Service Order

34   Salop is an old abbreviation for Shropshire, sometimes used on envelopes or telegrams, and comes from the Anglo-French "Salopesberia". It is normally replaced by the more contemporary "Shrops" although Shropshire residents are still referred to as "Salopians."

35   Napooed—all over, finished, done for, ruined or inoperative. Derived from a pronunciation of the French 'il n'y a plus' - 'there is no more'.

Gunner Gullet wrote:

> "As we walked home on Sunday [at Larkhill] the clear heavens sounded with the hum and boom of dozens of aeroplanes. Great flying schools are in the neighbourhood. We walk out on to one of these grounds and are cordially invited to look closely at a machine which has just alighted. One of us asked if many of the beginners were killed.
>
> "'None this week,' replied a young officer.
>
> "Life is very cheap in Europe to-day, and nowhere as cheap as in the heroic air service. Two Queensland boys, who came over with us, applied this week to the Colonel for a transfer to the Flying Corps. The Colonel is not partial to transfers. 'Do you know if there are any vacancies?' he asked.
>
> "'There ought to be,' one of them promptly replied. 'We counted twenty-three killed in 'The Times' casualty list last week.'
>
> "The Colonel surrendered. 'I'll see what can be done,' he said."[36]

On Friday February 22nd 1918, Lieutenant Palstra went up in an aeroplane for the first time. It was a De Havilland 6,[37] The Airco DH.6 was a British military trainer biplane known to the airmen by several nicknames, including the "Clutching hand" and "Skyhook".[38]

---

36   Healesville and Yarra Glen Guardian (Vic. : 1900 - 1942) Saturday 25 August 1917 Page 1, by Gunner HS Gullett."

37   Not to be confused with the much later "de Havilland Canada DHC-6 Twin Otter"

38   Other nicknames for the DH-6 included "crab," "clockwork mouse," and "flying coffin".

DH 6 biplane. Source: Wikipedia 'Airco DH6', retrieved Nov 15, 2016

It was a dual flight—Will's instructing pilot, who occupied the seat directly behind him, was Lieutenant Harper, A.F.C. Many biplanes had two cockpits, one on front of the other. This was useful for flying training. The instructor pilot sat in the rear cockpit so he could see what the student was doing in the front cockpit. In wartime, the dual configuration also meant that the pilot could fly the plane, while the passenger could focus on either observation and photography, or machine gunning and bombing.

Being February, the weather was wintry. Cold air was good for flying, especially in those early days of aviation. On cool days the air is dense, and produces more lift for the same speed. Aircraft need to go faster to get off the ground on a hot day than on a cool day, and that requires more power.

First Flight

Imagine lieutenants Harper and Palstra striding out onto that Shropshire airfield, wearing their heavy flying gear. Other pilots and cadets can be seen heading for their own machines.

Behind piled-up clouds in the west, the afternoon sun is falling towards the horizon. A few stray sunbeams tinge the scene with a blushing glow. The shadows of a row of parked biplanes stretch out across the gravelled aerodrome.

As Harper and Palstra draw near their aircraft, the safety crew, clad in grease-stained overalls, move away from it and wish them a cheery good morning. "All ship shape, gentlemen," affirms the chief mechanic.

The two aviators perform their own safety checks on the aircraft before climbing into their respective cockpits. With gloved hands they pull on their helmets and goggles. The noise of the aeroplane's engine will be deafening, so pilot and passenger will communicate by means of wired telephone equipment held in place under their flying helmets.

The groundsman stands in front of the biplane with both hands on the propeller.

Lieutenant Harper shouts "Contact!" The man pulls back hard on the wooden blades and they slowly commence to rotate. He steps back as the engine sputters noisily to life, and the spinning of the blades accelerates. They're moving so fast now that they seem to blur into a gossamer disc attached to the nose cone. Exhaust pipes pump out a billowing fog of choking gases.[39]

The cacophony of the aero engines increases as the training squadron's other planes fire up. Harper pulls the throttle back, and the noise of the engine rises to a constant bellow. The biplane, after a small lurch, moves forward across the airfield to the runway, turns around and begins its run, gathering speed. It races along the ground, jolting, until, when it's going fast enough, Harper pulls back on the throttle. All of a sudden the wheels are no longer touching the ground. . . smoothly the world falls away behind, and they're climbing 1,000 feet into the air.[40]

There is no feeling like this!

---

39   Inspired by a passage in 'Sagittarius Rising' by Cecil Lewis.

40   Inspired by: Early Birds—An Informal Account of the Beginnings of Aviation—J. Halpern. E.P. Dutton, New York, 1981.

It can be imagined that, as he soared into the sky, Cadet Lieutenant Palstra felt charged, from his toes to the roots of his hair, by a thrill he'd never known before. Flying was ecstasy. He realised, with joy, that he had discovered, at long last, 'the thing'—the job he was born to do.[41]

Will was the first person in his family to fly. Indeed, he was among the first few hundred human beings ever to do so. So excited was he about this event that he recorded the aircraft's number in his diary (No C9344), along with the details of the flight.

> "Course: SHAWBURY Drome to TERNHILL Drome 11 miles.
> Time out 4.50 p.m.—4.58 p.m. Time back 5.30 p.m.—6 p.m.
> Height 3000 ft. Wind at 3000—50 mph."

Any cadets who were not suited to flying generally opted out of the course during the dual flying training phase. There was a drop-out rate of around 45%—not surprising, given the dangerous and hair-raising nature of aviation in those days.

This first flight was a kind of test, to find out whether prospective pilots had the stomach for actual flying. Lieutenant Palstra passed with great success. On the day after his first flight with Lieutenant Harper, he was posted to A Flight, No 5 Training School A.F.C. under Captain Wrigley.[42]

Wrigley tutored Will in the basics of flying a biplane. His student must have performed well, or it might have been part of cadet training to experience different aircraft, because on 8 March Captain Wrigley told Will he was to change from De Havillands to Avros.

---

41   Will's mother wrote in a letter of reply to him dated 22.4.18, "I am so pleased you feel you have struck 'the thing'... I never thought that this would mean 'flying' but all the same what ever it is, it is in a way like a burden from my heart, that at last you feel happy in the work you are engaged in and feel you can put all your energies into it..."

42   After the war, Captain Wrigley wrote a history of No. 3 Squadron's war experience, entitled, "The Battle Below".

After telling him this, Captain Wrigley went up with another pupil at 10 a.m., lost control of the aeroplane's propeller and crashed in a ploughed field, damaging the undercarriage and propeller.

"No more instruction that day," Will succinctly wrote in his diary.

Captain Wrigley had done very well, to be able to walk away from such an accident in one piece, but the crash-landing must have seriously rattled him, because the following day Will reported, "Beautiful day, but Wrigley is not taking up pupils. There is a rumour about him going away."

Wrigley was made of stern stuff, however, and remained.

On Tuesday 2nd April No. 5 Training Squadron moved from Shawbury to RAF Minchinhampton in the county of Gloucestershire, where it joined the 1st Wing A.F.C.

Will wrote,

> "The Aerodrome occupied by No 5 & No 6 Squadrons is still under construction and quarters for the Officers are found at Hyde House, a big empty country mansion wearing a rather neglected appearance."

On 7th April, 1918, he made his first solo flight. Later he recorded in his 'War Experiences',

> ". . . I find on reference to my log book that I received my first dual instruction at Shawbury on 26th February 1918, and did my first solo flight at Minchinhampton on the 7th April. My flying instruction between these dates amounted to 6 hours 55 minutes."

Flying solo

From Will's diary of Sunday 7th April, 1918:

"Went up with Cole at 7 a.m. and did landings for 45 minutes. Made a few good landings, and at 7.45 a.m. after another good landing Cole got out of the bus, and asked if I felt confident to go on my own i.e. 'Solo'. With a little inward trepidation I nevertheless assured him I felt I could manage O.K. I removed the telephone from under my leather flying cap. Cole swung the prop. 'Switch off, petrol on'. 'Petrol off' and finally 'Contact!'

"The engine picked up almost immediately, Cole waved a farewell, and with the MONO of D 141 doing about 1050 revs per min., I gathered speed across the drome, eased the stick back gently, and—a look over the side of the bus assured me I was in the air and on my own for the first time.

"The 'take off' was excellent, and I flew west over the hangars, rapidly climbing to 2000 ft. Here I essayed a left turn then a right. Switched off the engine and did some glides for 1000 ft. I had kept the Drome within sight, but suddenly noticed that had lost it somehow. Picked it up after 2 minutes search. [It looked] Like a small farm some 3000 feet below and 4 miles away due North. Glided in for about half a mile and landed safely in the drome after a slightly 'dud' landing. No damage done however. I had been up alone exactly 25 minutes and put up a highly successful and creditable performance."

Will's training continued throughout April 1918. His dual flights included "Forced landings and contour chasing". His solo flights included practise at spins and turning while gliding. It was vital for military pilots to be skilled at manoeuvring in order to escape from enemy planes and groundfire, or, in the case of fighter planes, engaging in 'dogfighting'.

On days when strong winds, snow, fog or other atmospheric conditions prevented flying, Will wrote a single word in his diary: "Dud."

Few flight instruments were available for these early aircraft. There was a mere handful of basic gadgets on their instrument panels, such as an altimeter, an airspeed indicator, and a magnetic compass/heading indicator. They may also have had a vertical speed indicator, an attitude indicator with an artificial horizon, and a turn co-ordinator.

In 1918, all pilots were navigating visually. The instruments that would allow 'flying blind' had not yet been fully developed. This meant that pilots had to navigate and orientate the plane, estimate its distance above the ground and guess its distance from other aircraft, solely by reference to the landscape features they could see around them. If they flew into dense cloud, or if the cloud base came down and enveloped them, cutting off vision, there would be no way of knowing how close to the ground they were, or whether another aircraft was about to collide, or even if the plane was flying upside down. All-weather flying was risky. If landmarks were obliterated by clouds, fog, or snow for example, pilots could easily become lost.

This happened to Will.

At 9.30 on the morning of 20th April, Lieutenant Palstra left the 'Drome' at Minchinhampton, flying solo in an Avro D 141. He climbed through the clouds to an altitude of 10,000 feet then began to spiral down. In passing through a succession of thick cloud banks, he lost his way. When he emerged below the cloud layer he had no idea where he was, and intently scanned the countryside below, looking for any sign of a landmark.

It is remarkably easy to become lost when flying an aeroplane without modern navigational aids. Landscapes can look utterly different when you see them from a great height.

Eventually Will spotted a town and recognised it as Malmsbury. Now that he had his bearings he turned his flying machine toward home, only to discover that two cylinders refused to fire. The revs of his engine fell from 1050 to 850.

What was he to do?

He could have sought the nearest field where he could safely land the plane, but this was a risky business. Stone fences or unseen obstacles hidden in long grass, could spell catastrophe. Instead, he decided to try and go on.

He made it as far as Leighterton Aerodrome, where he landed at 11 a.m. From the aerodrome he telephoned a message to his 'Home Drome' and left the Leighterton mechanics fixing up the engine while he enjoyed lunch with No 8 Training Squadron, A.F.C.

At 2.30 p.m. his plane was declared fit to fly and he took off, but mechanical problems immediately showed up again. One cylinder was 'missing' or misfiring, so he turned around and landed back at Leighterton. The mechanics made another attempt to fix the engine and at 3 p.m. Will took off for a second time. On this occasion the engine worked as it should, but by the time he'd reached an altitude of 1000 feet, he ran into a snowstorm. With visibility dangerously reduced, he was forced to land yet again and stay with No 8 Training Squadron for the night.

Next morning he was up at 6 a.m. waiting for the weather to clear. The wind was in the east. Snow and continuous low mist blanketed the landscape.

By 2.30 p.m. the sky looked slightly clearer so, taking his leave of the boys at Leighterton, Will took off and pointed his machine north-east for home. Thick clouds floated in a layer at 500 feet, so he flew at an altitude of 300 to 400 feet all the way home. Visibility was poor. Fortunately his sharp eyes picked out a train track.

"Vision of ground very hazy and limited. Struck railway at Hayley Wood and followed it along the Golden Valley and so home."

As the month drew to a close, so Will's training came to an end. On Thursday 2nd May he wrote in his diary, "20 mins Dual landings with Cole for Pup. at 1025 a.m. At 11 a.m. took up Sopwith Pup A6159 Solo for 40 minutes. Made a successful flight and two landings thereby graduating.

"Time Solo to Graduation 13 hrs 15 mins. Time in air to Graduation 26 hrs 25 mins."

Will graduated as a Pilot on 2nd May, 1918, Pilot Certificate No. 13002 C.F.S. Royal Air Force and transferred to the Australian Flying Corps (A.F.C.).

Sopwith Pup. Source: Wikimedia commons, retrieved 30 Sept 2023

A Fully Fledged Pilot

What breed of men were they, Lieutenant Palstra and his brother pilots in 1918? F. M. Cutlack, author of 'The Australian Flying Corps 1914-1918' wrote,

'. . .this new field of war in the air offered considerable scope to the daring and initiative of the individual . . . The supreme qualities demanded of a pilot were youth, sound senses and good nerves: thus equipped, he might, if he lived, acquire all else needed from flying experience. . .

. . . a safe pilot was not necessarily a good fighting airman. Besides the pilot's ordinary qualifications, there was required for the fighting airman just that little more which may best be described as "devil". It means not so much recklessness as nice [precise] judgement of the moment's risks while simultaneously flying and fighting; sustained courage and determination without hot-headedness; unruffled confidence founded in perfect knowledge of his machine's capacity, estimation of the enemy's ability, and assurance of his own.'[43]

---

43   Cutlack: 'The Australian Flying Corps 1914-1918'

After graduation, Will enthusiastically practised flying in a variety of aeroplanes including Avros, Sopwith Pups and Sopwith Camels, and later, S.E.5s and R.E.8s.

Artillery Cooperation

Lieutenant Palstra had qualified as an air force pilot, but he decided not to fly fighter planes. In the light of his early discussions with his Salvation Army parents about becoming a medical officer instead of a combatant, it's likely that he knew that Mum and Dad would not relish the idea of their son dropping bombs on enemy troops, and machine-gunning enemy planes. Instead, he chose the equally (if not more) dangerous role of artillery cooperation pilot. He knew how vital this role was. He had, after all, once been an infantryman dependent on aeroplanes accurately pinpointing his battalion's position, so that the British artillery batteries could rain protective fire on the enemy and not on their own men.

In an interview with the commanding officer of 1st Wing A.F.C., Colonel Watt on 7th June at RAF Minchinhampton, Lieutenant Palstra applied to fly two-seater aircraft doing artillery cooperation work. His request was granted. Ten days later Will was transferred from No 5 Training Squadron to No 7 Training Squadron Leighterton, where he became the pilot of an R.E.8.

According to the Australian War Memorial's website, "Two main types of aircraft were used by the AFC: two-seater reconnaissance planes, in which the observer, armed with machine-guns, sat behind the pilot; and single-seater fighters. The latter dominated the popular imagination: they were the aces, the fastest aircraft fighting duels with men like themselves above the trenches. In reality, aerial combat was a difficult skill to master, requiring split-second timing and complete mastery of aircraft and weapons."[44]

The work Will had just volunteered for was highly dangerous, yet in the eyes of the public it was associated with slightly lower status than the job of flying fighter aeroplanes.

---

44   Australian War Memorial: Australian Military History: An overview. The Australian Flying Corps

In fact, the most important roles of military aviators during the First World War were reconnaissance (searching for useful military information in the field, especially by scrutinizing and photographing the ground), artillery cooperation (directing artillery and mortar fire onto a target), and 'contact patrol' (aircraft giving immediate support to infantry).

Michael Duffy in his article "The War in the Air—Observation and Reconnaissance" wrote, "The number of sorties flown on these missions far outweighed the number of missions flown on all other missions combined. It was more important, if less romantic, for a fighter pilot to shoot down an observation plane than to shoot down another fighter. More than half of Manfred von Richthofen's record-setting 80 victories were scored against reconnaissance and observation planes."[45]

'Observers' were airmen who took a back seat in the two-seater planes to perform reconnaissance, artillery cooperation and contact patrol missions. On reconnaissance missions the observer would carry a camera. Once the plane had reached the target territory, the pilot would tilt it on an angle, so that the observer could lean out the side and snap photographs. After the camera was brought back to base the photos would be developed and fitted together like a jigsaw puzzle to create a map of the enemy's trench network.

Michael Duffy wrote, "Reconnaissance missions were dangerous. They were usually carried out by a crew of two. The pilot was required to fly straight and level to allow the observer to take a series of overlapping photographs. There was no better target for anti-aircraft guns, no easier prey for stalking fighters."[37]

When planes were flying on artillery cooperation missions, the pilot and observer would look out for enemy artillery units that were hidden from their own gunners. They would then attempt to let their batteries know the location of the enemy. Communication was a problem, because reliable ground to air "wireless" radio contact for aeroplanes had not yet

---

45 "The War in the Air—Observation and Reconnaissance." www.firstworldwar.com/airwar/observation.htm 37 www.firstworldwar.com/airwar/observation.htm "The War in the Air—Observation and Reconnaissance" 38 Aviation in World War I—Wikipedia, the free encyclopedia

been fully developed. "After March 1915, a two-seater on 'artillery observation' duties was typically equipped with a primitive radio transmitter transmitting the dots and dashes of a Morse key, but had no receiver." [46]

This meant that communication between artillery batteries and moving aeroplanes relied mostly on visual signals.

Airmen on "contact patrol" had to fly over the battlefield while fighting was in progress, while simultaneously communicating with the advancing infantry. Messages had to be passed back and forth using crude methods such as sounding a Klaxon horn and dropping messages from the aeroplane. This was made even more difficult because, "Soldiers were naturally reluctant to reveal their positions to aircraft, as it was difficult for them to distinguish between friend and foe."[47]

On 20th June Lieutenant Palstra was posted to "C" Flight, where he continued to train with Captain H. N. Wrigley. All was going well until 23rd June, when on a half-hour solo flight, he narrowly escaped death.

He had climbed his aeroplane to an altitude of 1000 feet and was just beginning to make a left-hand turn. The engine torque was very strong, and suddenly he went into a spin. Spins can be difficult to pull out of, and are often lethal. His flying machine pivoted about six times, falling hundreds of feet in a very short time, before he managed to get it to flatten out at 500 ft.

This unnerving experience was made even more frightening by the thought that pilots had been killed doing spins in RE8s when the wing extensions broke under the pressure. "These R.E.8s have a nasty habit of smashing their extensions, so—no more spins," Will wrote in his diary.

Piloting biplanes was a terribly dangerous occupation. At RAF Leighterton on 3rd July 1918 two more men lost their lives flying an R.E.8.

---

46 https://military-history.fandom.com/wiki/Aviation_in_World_War_I

47 Aviation in World War I - Wikipedia, the free encyclopedia

Will wrote in his diary,

> "3.7.18 Poor old Thompson has killed himself and his passenger, a mechanic. Dived steeply at a target. Dive too long. Yanked her out of dive with engine. Extensions collapsed in mid air. Crashed to ground at about 200 mph. Burst into flames. Burnt to a cinder.
>
> Moral—beware of those extensions."

As with the B.E.2e aeroplane, the long extensions on the upper wings of RE8s were reputed to be liable to collapse if the aircraft was dived too sharply. On 5th July 5.7.18 Will was one of the pall bearers at Thompson's funeral. Two days later there was yet another training fatality.

> "7.7.18 Stronach, a nice little fellow, spins into ground on first solo.
>
> Broke his neck."

Will did not lose his nerve, and despite his poor health and the shocking accidents that occurred to his comrades, he carried on. By 16th July he had completed his final test on piloting RE8s and he was ready to be transferred to the Artillery and Infantry Co-operation School at Winchester.

Will with an aeroplane. Photo from family archives. Written on back of photo in Will's handwriting: 'R.E.8 Title of picture: "Machines I have flown—and bust". I wiped off the rear(?) undercarriage of this dear old bus in landing her. She has since come out of hospital looking none the worse. Bill'

Meanwhile Will's brother Charles continued to endure the unremitting horror of heavy trench warfare. It is clear that that his war experiences, year after year, from Gallipoli to the Somme, had taken a serious toll on his physical and mental health. He had seen terrible sights. He had been wounded more than once. When he enlisted way back in 1914, he'd probably thought he'd be home by Christmas. After years of unimaginable stress, he was struggling to cope. It was hard enough to survive, let alone pick up a pen and put it to paper. His letters to his parents were few and far between.

The Kaiserschlacht

Will was preparing to fly into the conflict on the front line at an extremely dangerous period of the war.

Near the end of 1917 and during the early months of 1918, the Germans had been gathering and training a special force for a new offensive they called "The Kaiserschlacht" (The Kaiser's Battle)[48]. These forces numbered around 900,000 men (74 divisions), and included stormtroopers, elite assault units, and specialist artillery and mortar batteries.

The majority of the men in this special force were well-rested. Their morale was high and they had a keen desire to fight. Germany's General von Ludendorff provided them with plenty of new and advanced weapons, and had them trained in the new German offensive tactics that had proved so successful toward the close of 1917.

Von Ludendorff focussed this force along a 50-mile (80km) battle-front between Bapaume and St Quentin in the Somme Sector of Northern France – a front that was currently held by 30 British divisions (around 40,000 men). His idea was to crush the British and take control of the Channel ports before the American troops had time to arrive in greater numbers. He reasoned that if this could be done, the Germans would be in a better position to negotiate favourable terms when the war ended. He planned to execute the offensive in a series of blows.

---

48   This was also known as "The 1918 Spring Offensive".

The British guessed that the enemy would probably mount an assault like this in the spring of 1918. Milder weather provided good flying conditions, and air reconnaissance and observation had become a vital component of offensives.

Following the catastrophic defeats of late 1917, however, the British army was struggling. They had lost huge numbers of troops. Field Marshal Haig was commanding considerably fewer than he had in early 1917, and many of these men were young conscripts still in their teens, or older men in their late forties. Reinforcements were trickling in at a slow pace. Due to the carnage of late 1917, the British government was cautiously restraining men who showed a desire to enlist; many people now viewed the generals as "wasteful".

The Allies had to spread themselves thinly along the front. The French army had been weakened by mutinies in 1917, and the Americans had not yet arrived in full force. All things considered, the Allies were in a very unfavourable position to meet a resolute attack.

It was just before dawn on the 21st March 1918 that the Germans struck. They deployed 700 aircraft in support of the ground troops on that first day of the Kaiserschlacht. The outcome was horrendous for the British. Their front line was almost completely smashed, and more than 20,000 troops were forced to surrender. The casualty rate was horrifically high, and they had no option but to retreat.

Artillery and Infantry Co-operation School

In the last days of July 1918 Will shook hands with his comrades at No 7 Training Squadron Leighterton, bade them goodbye and departed. At 9:15pm on 29th July he arrived at the Artillery and Infantry Co-operation School, Winchester, where he was posted to Course #58.

Will wrote nothing in his diary between his arrival at Winchester on 29th July and 17th August, the day he finished the course. He was probably too busy to record events. His exam results were excellent and he was justly proud of them.

From Will's Diary:

> "17.8.18 End of course at A & ICS Winchester. Put up wings as Service Pilot."

'Putting up wings' seems to indicate that at this time Lieutenant Palstra was issued with his AFC officers' service dress uniform, which sported a pair of 'AFC' pilot's wings embroidered above the left breast pocket of the khaki wool gabardine tunic. The tunic was also fitted with brass Australian Military Forces buttons, general service 'Rising Sun' collar badges, the officer's rank insignia and curved 'AUSTRALIA' shoulder titles. AFC colour patches were sewn onto both upper sleeves.

In his aviator's clothing, Will would have attracted attention and admiration everywhere he went.

The AFC's uniform was similar to that of the Royal Flying Corps. RFC pilot Cecil Lewis wrote, "To belong to the RFC in those days was to be singled out among the rest of the khaki-clad world by reason of the striking double-breasted tunic, the Wings, the little forage-cap set over one ear, but more than this by the glamour surrounding the "birdmen". Flying was still something of a miracle. We who practised it were thought very brave, very daring, very gallant: we belonged to a world apart. In certain respects it was true, and though I do not think we traded on this adulation, we could not but be conscious of it."[49]

---

49   Sagittarius Rising' by Cecil Lewis

Will with AFC wings, 1918

Now that he was fully trained, Will took a job as a ferry pilot with the Central Despatch Pool RAF whilst awaiting a vacancy overseas. He spent the next few weeks ferrying flying machines from various parts of England to France, then catching a boat back to England.

It was not until September that his new orders came through.

"9.9.18 Arrive C.D.P. 10 p.m. Instructed to report to A.I.F. Headquarters for overseas, as Col. Watt has asked for me.

"10.9.18 Reported A.I.F. Headquarters & (Bolo) Room 29 Air Ministry Cecil Hotel. To go overseas next morning."

Back on the Front Line

The Hindenburg Line and The Battle of Mont St Quentin

While Will was ferrying aeroplanes for the CDP, on the Western Front the enemy had retreated from a series of crushing defeats. Their entire line was moving backwards, and at last the Allies appeared to be getting the upper hand.

The Germans, however, prepared to make a stand when they reached Peronne and Mont Saint-Quentin, near the German "Siegfriedstellung" (the Hindenburg Line).

The four-day Battle of Mont Saint-Quentin then ensued (31 Aug 1918 – 3 Sept 1918).

In the end, Britain and her allies triumphed. The taking of Mont St Quentin and Péronne came to be regarded as among the finest Australian feats on the Western Front. The Allies beat back the Germans, who, by 4th September, had retreated to the outer defences of the so-called "Hindenburg Outpost-Line" that lay on that high ground over the St Quentin Canal.

The Hindenburg Line was the last and strongest of the German army's defences. Built in 1916, it was a heavily fortified zone running several miles behind the active front. It was not in fact a single line, but a series of up to six lines of defence across a zone about 6,000 yards (5.5km) wide, laced with miles of barbed wire and studded with concrete gun emplacements.

Here in this network of abandoned, weed-infested British trenches, riddled with long, impenetrable thickets of barbed wire, the retreating Germans dug themselves in. Their resistance grew stronger, so that during September 8th and 9th the advance of the Allies slowed.

No. 3 Squadron, Australian Flying Corps

In France on 10th September 1918, Will was posted to No. 3 Squadron, Australian Flying Corps, "Contact" Flight.

No. 3 Squadron consisted of "A", "B" and "C" Flights. Each Flight was made up of six officers who were pilots, five air mechanics and a corporal. There were also various support personnel, such as a cook.

This squadron was sometimes described as the 'maid-of-all-work' squadron due to the large number of different functions it fulfilled. Its pilots flew on many photography missions in addition to performing reconnaissance 'contact patrols' and providing support for troops on the ground. One day they might be flying low over enemy lines to find out what the Germans were up to; next day they might be dropping bombs, or swooping on an enemy plane with machine guns blazing.

The Red Baron

Early in April 1918, five months before Will's arrival, No. 3 Squadron had received the executive order to move to the Somme front in France.

Here, on 21st April 1918, the celebrated German pilot Manfred Baron von Richthofen was shot down by ground fire. He was flying the red Fokker triplane that had earned him the name of the Red Baron. Richthofen's body and the remains of his aircraft were recovered that night by a party of mechanics from No. 3 Squadron, AFC. Next day he was buried with full military honours, including a firing party provided by the Squadron. The grave was marked with an inscription in both English and German, as follows:

"Cavalry Captain Mannfred Baron von Richthofen

Age 25 years, killed in action, aerial combat near SAILLY_LE_ SEC SOMME, FRANCE, 21st April 1918"

In search of the squadron

Numerous small aerodromes were scattered all over France. They all possessed at least one landing strip of course, but due to the exigencies of war, not all of them possessed hangars for the planes, or hutments to shelter the men, or proper latrines, or much equipment at all. The runways were generally surfaced with grass or dirt. Sometimes they were paved with a little asphalt.

As the front line moved erratically back and forth, No. 3 Squadron Australian Flying Corps moved its aerodrome base from place to place, keeping always just within the Allied side of the line so that they were situated on friendly ground but close enough to enemy ground to take part in the action. Due to the nomadic nature of the squadron, the whereabouts of its headquarters at any given time was not always known to rail transport officers, whose job it was to direct troops to their destinations.

After landing in France, Lieutenant Palstra caught a train to Canaples. It was there that he met two other graduate pilots destined for No. 3 Squadron, Tait and Frazer. The three of them were forced to stay at Canaples overnight, because the R.T.O. (Rail Transport Officer) could not tell them where their squadron was.

In fact, on 6 September, No.3 had taken advantage of the lull in fighting due to the retreat to move from its aerodrome north of the bombed city of Amiens, up to the village of Proyart.

Will and his comrades set off in search of the squadron. From Will's Diary:

"13.9.18 . . . Left Amiens by train at 8.30 p.m. Passed through Villers Bretonneax. Arrived Laflaques 11 p.m. Slept the night in hut abandoned by the Hun on his retreat as R.T.O. was again blissfully ignorant of the whereabouts of the Squadron.

"14.9.18 Set out on foot to find the Squadron. Walked East along the Amiens - St Quentin road and struck the Drome of No 3 Squadron A.F.C. about a mile north of this road and East of Proyart. Reported, and had a much needed wash and breakfast. Posted to "C" Flight Contact Patrol. Flight Commander Captain Brierly, D.F.C. C.O. Squadron Major Blake."

In a letter to his parents he wrote:
"I have been posted to "C" Flight which does all the low flying work of the Squadron, finding out the position of our own and the enemy's infantry, machine gunning, bombing, etc., and is considered quite the stunt flight of the Squadron. We work with the Australian Corps, which means that I shall actually be flying over Charles."

Whether due to constant bombing of buildings or whether the aerodrome was too rudimentary and transitory to possess hutments, the pilots at Proyart were quartered in tents. The aeroplanes, being more fragile and easily blown away, were housed in hangars. These were not hangars built of wood or steel, however; they were made of canvas.

Will wrote about the scenes he witnessed when he arrived at Proyart:

> "The Officers of the Squadron I found in tents, two to a tent, and so my chum and I immediately decided to go on a foraging expedition in order to suitably furnish our happy home.
>
> "The whole of this district has been taken from the Hun in the recent push, and the countryside for miles around is covered with newly constructed huts and dugouts, all in excellent condition, (and other) material abandoned by the Hun in his ignominious and precipitous retreat.
>
> "We found Hun dugouts of wonderfully comfortable construction close handy from which could be salvaged chairs enough to fill the Melbourne town hall. We also carefully selected an oak table, beds, chairs, shaving mugs, glasses, and a candlestick. Things looked very nice and comfortable.
>
> "I went to see a 15" Little Bertha gun about 200 yards from the 'Drome. Before abandoning it to the 3rd Battalion, A.I.F. the Hun had smashed the barrel with a charge of H.E. (high explosive), bursting it at the breech. . . .
>
> This gun was evidently intended for bombarding Amiens."

As soon as possible after he arrived, Will got into an aeroplane and took off.

> "Did some "sandbag" landings. Smashed centre section wires on first machine owing to landing in a small depression. Made 4 good landings on another machine."
>
> Take my first trip along the line tomorrow at 10 a.m. Lieutenant Hamilton, observer for Flight Commanders, is to show me round."

Lieutenant Ernest Devlin-Hamilton[50] was to become a close associate of Will's.

Up till now, whenever Lieutenant Palstra had piloted an aeroplane it had been over peaceable lands. He was soon to know what it was like to be shot at while airborne. 'Archie' was a British military slang word for German anti-aircraft fire. Will's flight companion, Lieutenant Hamilton, would also give back what the enemy gave them.

His plane soared over war-torn France, following the Hindenberg Line. In his diary, the names of French towns and villages now come thick and fast. He seems to literally thrive on the danger and excitement.

In the forthcoming conflict, flying "artillery cooperation", Will would pilot the squadron's two-seater R.E.8s, rather than the fighting "scouts", (which were single-seater machines of small size, high speed, rapid manoeuvring ability, and eventually equipped with forward armament of double machine-guns).

Despite the lack of forward-mounted machine guns, Will's aircraft could deliver a lethal rain on the enemy. His observer Devlin-Hamilton, in the seat behind, operated a Lewis gun, which he could fire over the side, while Will tilted the wings for him to get a clear shot.

From Will's Diary:

"15.9.18 Took off on R.E.8 B/4048 (S) at 10.10 a.m. with Lieutenant Hamilton as observer. Flew down Amiens – St Quentin Road to Vermand, thence to Bihecourt, the Southern Boundary of our Corps front.   Got

Archied within first few minutes of being over the line. Zigzagged and Archie soon shut up. Flew along the line at 3000 feet till I got the hang of it. Then descended to 800 feet and had a closer look. Enemy machine guns opened up on us south of Le Verguier. Hamilton engaged them with his Lewis gun. We machine gunned the line right down to Bihecourt.

---

50   Lieutenant Ernest Alexander Devlin-Hamilton, No. 3 Squadron, Australian Flying Corps, First World War, 1914-1918. Recommended for the Distinguished Flying Cross, 29 January 1919.

"Flew down the Somme over Roisel, Tincourt to Peronne. Engineers are busy building new steel bridges over the river. Peronne is badly knocked about. From here followed the Canal de la Somme to Amiens, and along the St Quentin Road home. Could see St Quentin clearly from 1000 feet this morning."

The thunderstorm

The enemy was not the only threat to aviators.

Just before dawn on the morning of the 17th September, a violent thunderstorm, accompanied by a cyclonic gale, swept over the countryside and caused considerable damage. It tore to ribbons the canvas hangars of No. 3 Squadron. All the squadron's aircraft were damaged, a number of them seriously. Some planes had their backs broken by heavy steel tent-poles falling across the fuselages, leaving them beyond repair. Others suffered repairable damage to wings, ailerons and rudders. Three aircraft for which there was no hangar accommodation, and which had been pegged down in the open, sustained the least damage.

Only their ailerons (the hinged flight control surfaces forming part of the trailing edge of each wing) were slightly bent, because the control columns of the aircraft had been insecurely fastened, allowing them to flap about in the wind.

Of this event Will wrote,

"At 2 a.m. this morning a terrific cyclone passed over this Drome. I was awakened by the moaning of the wind, and almost before I could let down the flaps of the tent the hurricane burst on us.

"In less than a minute the tent came down with a crash of top of Tait and myself, exposing us to the full deluge of rain. We grabbed hold of the edge of the canvas and endeavoured to drag it flat over us and our belongings. In this we were partially successful. At any rate we managed to keep our blankets fairly dry.

"For half an hour we lay there underneath the flattened tent. Then the storm abated, and wet to the skin and in the dark we proceeded to erect our flimsy domicile. The contents of my tin trunk were about the only dry things we had left. From amongst these I fished out dry underclothing for Tait and self, and went to sleep again.

"The light of morning disclosed a wonderful orgy of wreckage and confusion. Nearly every tent had been blown down and the contents strewn over the landscape. Letters, maps, books, clothes, including my own were jumbled together in a sopping and muddy mass. Unfortunately the hangars had suffered and also the machines in them. By 9 a.m. there were only 3 machines serviceable out of 18.

"Happily the morning turned out sunny with a fair breeze, and soon everywhere blankets and clothes were drying on lines constructed from Hun telephone wire. This wire is of steel with a coating of insulating material, and very strong (another proof of Germany's shortage of copper). The whole day has been spent in drying, sorting out sodden letters and maps, and re-rigging tents to withstand future onslaughts.

"8 p.m. We are once more comfortably established, everything is dry and the tent proof against a 100 mph blizzard. There is a stunt tomorrow when we hope to advance our line up to the old positions in front of the Hindenburg Line, or if favourable some 5000 yards from our present line.

The 1st & 4th Divisions A.I.F. are taking part on our Corps front."

As Will mentions, the attack on the Hindenburg Outpost-Line was scheduled for the following day.

In "The Battle Below", Captain Wrigley wrote, "In view of the offensive which was to commence the next day, this damage to aircraft was a very serious matter. The squadron's mechanics had to work hard all day on the 17th to repair the damage in readiness for the morrow. During a single day those dedicated men managed to repair most of the damage, while maintaining at least one aircraft in constant over the line throughout the hours of daylight. Two new aircraft were also flown in from the Aircraft Park. By nightfall the squadron had fifteen serviceable aircraft for the next day's battle, which speaks highly for the ability of both officers and mechanics."[51]

On the morning of 18 September, the 1st and 4th Australian Divisions launched a preliminary attack on the Hindenburg Line, as the opening of "The Grand Offensive".

---

51   Wrigley, The Battle Below.

Attack on the Hindenburg Line

The Australian War Memorial records that, "At 5.20 am, Lieutenant General Sir John Monash's troops, supported by huge artillery barrages, attacked the heavily fortified German defences and machine-gun posts. Using only eight tanks (as well as dummy tanks to distract the Germans), they broke through German positions and took 4,300 prisoners. Although there were 1,000 dead or wounded, this cost was fairly slim compared to the losses of the German forces." [52]

Among those AIF infantry divisions was Lieutenant Charles Palstra in the 46th Battalion.

Lieutenant Will Palstra was not among those who fought on 18 September. He had received other orders, and was fully occupied ferrying and testing aeroplanes. Knowing that

---

52   Australian War Memorial: The Hindenburg Line: Breaking the Hindenburg Line

Charles's battalion had been involved in the attack, Will took the earliest opportunity of a day's leave to head out in search of his brother in the 46th Battalion.

From Will's Diary:

"19.9.18 Set out this morning to get some news about Chas. Learnt from an officer from his Battalion I met near Le Mesnil that he had been wounded in the back of the head. Enquired for him at No 53 & 12 C.C.S. [Casualty Clearing Station] Le Chapelette, and finally found he had been admitted to No 55 C.C.S. at Doingt, but had left by Hospital train the same day, presumably for Boulogne. Was assured that the wound is not serious.

"Passed hundreds of Boche prisoners being marched to P.O.W. Camps.

The 1st & 4th Divisions A.I.F. have, it is stated, captured 5000 prisoners between them. Peel and Jeffers missing. Believed shot down in flames."

Cutlack wrote, "One of the machines engaged on photographic work did not return and its crew, lieutenants Peel and Jeffers, (observer), were never heard of again."

This could so easily be Will's fate, at any time. Dodging and diving in the skies over France, he faced extreme danger and non-stop action during the following days. As battles raged across the ground and in the air, he and Devlin-Hamilton soared into the skies, not only on artillery cooperation missions, but also on contact patrols, and photographic reconnaissance missions. They also bombed the enemy.

On the morning of 22 September Lieutenant Palstra was on 'Artillery Patrol' when he and his observer dropped five bombs on the Hindenburg Line and Bellicourt. Casually, he recorded in his diary, "Got heavily archied on way back."

The anti-aircraft fire cut his aeroplane's Petot tube in two, smashed the leading edge of the left top of the plane, and blasted two holes in the bottom left wing, and two holes in fuselage behind his observer in the rear cockpit.

In return for this damage to his aircraft, Will send down three N.F. calls on active hostile batteries. (N.F. stands for "Now Firing". It means an enemy battery has been spotted in action, and invites fire upon it.)

In a hair-raising morning's work Will also dodged one enemy Albatros Scout, and a formation of eight German Fokker Biplanes.

No. 3 Squadron was needed to support to the British IX Corps as it advanced alongside Australian troops to the starting line for the main offensive against the Hindenburg Line. This support would take the form of a night-time bomb attack on a German position, on 24 September. Lieutenant Palstra and his observer, Hamilton, were ordered to take part. They would be carrying four bombs in their aeroplane, to drop on the enemy. In retaliation, their flying machine would most likely be vigorously attacked by machine gun fire. Furthermore, they would have to take off in darkness, unable to see the landscape or the horizon. It would be about as dangerous as any "stunt" could get.

Perhaps it was the knowledge that the following day might be the last day of his life, that prompted Will to seek the company of his old comrades of the 39th on the eve of this attack.

> "23.9.18 Paid a visit to 39th Battalion at Bois des Flaques[53], north-east of Doingt. Found quite a number of the old officers there ... Had dinner with them... Afterwards about half a dozen of us went to see the "Coo-ees"—3rd Div. Concert Party—at Doingt and sat packed together from Brigadier Generals to plain Diggers enjoying a rattling entertainment for one and a half hours.

---

53   Bois des Flaques: literally, 'Wood of Puddles"

"Got home "Lorry hopping" about 10 p.m. just in time to get all the "oil" about the bombing stunt before dawn tomorrow."

Will must have promised his mates he would swoop down over the 39th Battalion's camp by way of greeting, the next day—if he survived the bombing raid.

From Will's War Experiences and diary:

"On the 24th September I was one of the six pilots ordered to bomb the enemy front line Pontruet-Gricourt before dawn.

"4.50 a.m. Moonlight, but dawn still far away.

"Aircraft took off . . . in complete darkness, a novel experience for all of us. The Flight Commander flashed an electric torch at the far end of the aerodrome, and we made for this in taking off.

"Took off with 4 bombs to bomb portion of Hun trenches between Pontevet and Gricourt, in cooperation with IX Corps Infantry, which is hopping over to take some more ground in front of the Hindenburg Line. Zero hour 5 a.m. Thick ground mist and much smoke made location of target very difficult. Also machine-gun Hun trenches.

"We had no navigation lights, no wingtip flares, and had to cruise up and down the Somme until dawn at 0630 hours waiting for sufficient light to land. All returned without accident."

"All 8 machines returned safely. My first experience of night flying."

Possibly Will was swept up by that euphoria that often accompanies an escape from danger, because he then recorded, "Took Captain Giles of 39th A.I.F. for a joy ride to Amiens by air. Also dived low on to 39th Camp."

"Bombing is quite a pastime here." Will wrote to his parents on 25th September;

> "Every clear night the Hun comes over, but seldom does much damage. During the past week our night flying scouts brought down five huge machines, so he is growing more cautious.
>
> "I have taken part in two bombing expeditions so far, one by day and one by night, both on a section of the famous Hindenburg Line. I scarcely know which is the most exciting. Archie gave us a close run for it on the day stunt, but flying at night is weird and eerie, with a barrage spouting up geysers of molten metal underneath. We had to get low enough to drop our bombs with accuracy on the Hun trenches, after which I got my observer to pump lead into Very light merchants.[54]
>
> "(26.9.18) The next day I attended an American Divisional conference, and on the invitation of the Yank General explained just what the aeroplane wanted from the infantry in a battle."

---

54   Very lights = flares

Will piloting an AFC aeroplane with a boomerang painted on the cowling.

Will with two fellow pilots, 1918

Will with his observer Devlin-Hamilton

S.E.5 Scout with kangaroo painted on the fuselage. One of many aeroplanes photographed and piloted by Will during his time with the AFC.

The Americans Advance

The United States had entered into the Great War in April 1917. By September 1918 the Americans were playing an important role in the conflict, and a pivotal battle was looming.

The Battle of St. Quentin Canal was to commence on 29 September 1918. It would involve British, Australian and American forces operating as part of the British Fourth Army.

C.W Bean tells us that, "The Australian Mission joined the Americans on September 24th. The full scheme of co-operation by the American and Australian Corps was expounded by Monash on the 26th at a conference attended by the heads and staffs of every formation taking part."

On 26th September 1918, Will accompanied his Commanding Officer to this conference with 106th Regiment, American Army. The conference took place in a small dugout near the line. Present were Major General O'Ryan of the U.S. Army, Brigadier General Brand of 1st A.I.F. Div. and some twenty American colonels all crowded together around a narrow table. They asked Lieutenant Palstra to have a say on the topic of contact patrol flares and, among other things, he laid stress on the lighting of flares to show the position of the troops as soon as the Klaxon was sounded by the patrolling aeroplane.

As mentioned earlier, at the beginning of the Great War planes were not outfitted with radios. Air-to-ground communication relied on visual aids such as the lighting of flares. This was effective for ground crews, but pilots had few ways to communicate back. They could drop flares, for example, or sound a Klaxon horn. The outbreak of war spurred the pace of invention, so that by early 1916 some airmen were using air-to-ground radio transmitters/receivers in the war over France. It appears that during this period Will's squadron, at least, did not have access to wireless radio, or else the instruments could not be relied upon in the heat of battle.

Will recorded, "The Americans advance tomorrow morning, bringing our line closer up to the Hindenburg Line."

The job of Lieutenant Palstra's unit was to fly 'contact' patrols in advance of the U.S. troops. The R.E.8, his aircraft of choice, was a well-armed machine. It was fitted with a Vickers gun for the pilot, which was mounted on the port side of the fuselage, with a synchronising mechanism to avoid shooting the propeller to pieces. In addition to the pilot's Vickers gun, one or two Lewis guns were mounted in the rear cockpit for the use of the observer or photographer. The R.E.8's other armaments included up to 224 lb (102 kg) of bombs.

At 6.50 am on 27th September, Lieutenant Palstra and his observer Lieutenant Hamilton took off from the airstrip at Bouvincourt on a 'contact' patrol to support the dawn attack on the Bellicourt-Vendhuile line by the 27th American Division.

Ground mist and smoke were obscuring the airmen's view of the landscape beneath the aeroplane. The cloud base hovered low, too, so Will had to fly at an altitude of only 300 feet to maximise his chances of discerning anything on the ground. Even in peacetime it is risky to fly so low. In wartime, it brings an aircraft within easy range of anti-aircraft fire.

From Will's "War Experiences"

"Anti-aircraft fire, especially machine gun fire, was heavy, bullets were continually striking some part of the aircraft, and the bad visibility and low height made it difficult for a beginner to get a proper perspective of the ground."

"Was fired at from the ground by everything that could be slung at us. Flaming onions[55] in strings, anti-tank guns, field guns, A.A. guns, a kind of mitrailleuse[56] firing a spray of incendiary bullets like a stream from a watering can, M.G. [machine gun] and rifle fire furioso."

In order to escape the enemy fire, Will had to perform some aerobatic manoeuvres in his "old bus" that were more suited to a lighter single-seater scout machine. He was "unable to lift the heavy R.E.8 into the friendly clouds above," so he "slung the machine about like a scout for about 10 minutes but got hit by bullets near the tail plane and through the prop."[57]

"It took beaucoup manoeuvring to avoid being hit, as a matter of fact the machine was hit in three places, but the damage was not vital."[58]

---

55   'Flaming onions' were produced by a Gatling - style five barrelled revolving 37 mm gun, used in the anti-aircraft role for low-level air defence up to about 5,000 feet. It was not specifically designed for this task but, used in this way, it fired a round from each of its five barrels in turn at a very high cyclical rate, the tracers from this giving the effect of a 'string of flaming onions.'" Jack Sheldon, http://1914- 1918.invisionzone.com/forums. 11 November 2008.

56   A mitrailleuse is a type of volley gun with multiple barrels of rifle calibre that can fire either multiple rounds at once, or several in rapid succession. [Wikipedia]

57   From Will's Diary, 27 September 1918

58   "Beaucoup manoeuvring" = a lot of manoeuvring. "The Australians had a few tags of soldier-French picked up from the villagers when the time and conditions were suitable… 'San fairy ann' (Ca ne fait rien), 'Beaucoup oofs (oeufs), 'Madame', 'Fromach' (fromage)… with occasionally such tours de force as 'Parti pour les tranchees', and 'Sacres Boches' or 'Australiens beaucoup brigands' were the small coin of this intercourse." (Bean, Vol. VI)

Palstra and Hamilton were unable to locate the American troops. To compound their dire situation, in searching for them they lost direction and ended up some 6000 yards (5.5km) on the wrong side of enemy territory, or 'Hunland'.

Although Hamilton was an experienced observer, in very little time neither he now Will had any idea where they were. For about a quarter of an hour they zigzagged across the skies above enemy territory, thoroughly lost and dodging a red-hot hail of bullets. Both airmen were, by now, in a state of terror. Though they had nerves of steel, they were not immune to fear.

This state of affairs continued until they recognised a small lake about five miles inside enemy territory which gave them a line of flight—the compass was useless because of the violent turns necessary.

Just before they crossed back over the front line into friendly territory, a German aircraft dived out of the clouds immediately ahead of them.

> "Suddenly ran into an Albatros Scout through the mist not 150 yards away," recorded Will. "Dug Hamilton in the ribs and yelled "HUN!" pointing in his direction. As our plane came from Hunland he was entirely unsuspecting and made no sign of having seen us. Kicked on right rudder doing a flat turn and got broadside on to him, thus giving Ham. a chance with his Lewis. Ham. who like myself had been in a blue funk up to now, rose to the occasion and rattled a drum of Lewis fair into the Hun while I kept position. He appeared to catch fire, large patches of smoke came from his machine and he went down in a sideslip dive. My first Hun."

After that they managed to regain their own side of the front line, but the weather changed, and conditions proved too difficult for flying. Lieutenants Palstra and Hamilton had to return to the aerodrome without fulfilling their mission.

Will recorded,

"That ground fire was pretty awful though, and both Hamilton and I felt we had done a day's work once we got back to our side of the line.

"On returning to the Drome, examination showed that one bullet had passed through the fuselage near the tail plane, another had smashed the leading edge of the propeller, whilst a piece of high explosive which had ripped the wing finally embedded itself in the woodwork of my seat. This latter bit cut a piece of steel plating clean in two and got very close to me. I have kept this piece of H.E. as a souvenir of my first Hun and a narrow squeak.[59]"

From Will's Diary:

"28.9.18 Took Lt. Pomray over the Line for Contact. Got machine-gunned from northern end of Canal tunnel. Smashed left bottom wing aileron and rib. Bullets through tail plane and one through fuselage behind me. New left wing required. Our guns are ceaselessly bombarding the Hindenburg Line. Field guns are very close up—1500 yds.

"Tomorrow the Entente will deliver the Hun what is hoped to be the most smashing blow ever struck on the Western front."

---

59 This jagged grey piece of metal is still in the possession of the family in Melbourne.

The Breaking of the Hindenburg Line

The Germans had been using the St Quentin Canal as an extra defensive barrier forward of the Hindenberg Line. It was one of the most heavily defended stretches of the Line.

On 29 September Australian and American troops spearheaded the pivotal Battle of St Quentin Canal, a conflict involving British, Australian, French and American forces. The objective was to break through the Hindenburg Line, which in this sector used the St Quentin Canal as part of its defences.

Lieutenant Palstra took part in the attack. His exploits were recorded in "Fire in the Sky: The Australian Flying Corps in the First World War" by Michael Molkentin.

That day, at 3.30 p.m. Will and his observer took off on "contact patrol", to ascertain the position of the 27th American Division. Enemy ground-crews fired at their aeroplane all the way from Vendhuile to the town of Bony[60], in the district of Saint-Quentin.

In Will's words,

"This mission gave me considerable difficulty because of the confused nature of the situation. . . I find from my log book that these missions were done at a height of 800 feet, and that I did all subsequent Contact Patrols from this height. The reason for this is that one could never rely on troops lighting flares, indeed these were seldom seen. It was therefore necessary to go sufficiently low to be able to differentiate with certainty between khaki [Allies] and field grey [Germans]."

800 feet is low flying indeed, well within artillery range and highly dangerous. Both khaki and field grey had been chosen as the colours of military uniforms in the Great War because of their ability to merge with the landscape. It took sharp eyes to spot them.

Cutlack observed, "The reconnaissance machines of No. 3 flew daringly low to do their work as far as it could be done, and were all much shot about by this ground-fire."

Two bullets pierced through the left lower wing of the biplane carrying Will and his observer Devlin-Hamilton. From their vantage point in the sky they could see numerous Allied tanks burning in front of the Line. While flying over Bony, they encountered a German two-seater aircraft. Immediately the two planes engaged in an aerial fight. Will manoeuvred his flying-machine, dodging and twisting, while Hamilton fired the machine gun at the enemy. At length the German plane fled, and the Australians, too, returned safely to base.

---

60   Note: Although the name of this town appears to refer to bones, it is derived from the French "bon", meaning "good". It's English equivalent would be "Bonny".

The Battle of St Quentin Canal achieved its objectives, resulting in the first full breach of the Hindenburg Line in the face of heavy German resistance. Combined with other attacks along the length of the line, the Allied successes were beginning to convince the German high command that there was little hope of an ultimate German victory.

"Bill" and "Ham" continued to fly patrols as the attacks continued. Every day they climbed into their cockpits, donned their helmets and goggles, and took off again, not knowing if they would ever return. Their aeroplanes were often quite seriously damaged by gunfire, but so far they had managed to survive.

Once they were machine-gunned by German troops positioned in Vendhuile and Bony.

Two shots blasted through the tail plane of their flying machine, one of which completely severed one left rudder control and almost severed the other left rudder control. Will appears to have been pretty blasé about his aircraft getting shot up to the extent that it was almost uncontrollable. In his diary he mentions the fact in passing, as if it were nothing important.

On the morning of 2 October 1918 Lieutenants Palstra and Hamilton were up on another routine contact patrol, flying over Sequehart, which on the previous day had been captured by the Allies.

From the air, they watched hundreds of German prisoners being marched back to the west. While seeking to establish the position of the most forward allied troops in this area, they suddenly spotted a line of men about a mile long, rising from the ground some 1000 yards ahead. Suspecting that this could be a German counterattack, Will pushed the control column forward and volplaned the plane down to 400 feet so that they could get a better look. He was right; the troops were clad in field grey.

Immediately Hamilton dropped a parachute flare to warn the "Diggers" and bring down an artillery barrage. The aviators also fired red Very-lights to attract other planes to this 'favourable target', and sent two wireless S.O.S. calls on sector.

In response to the red Verys, two Camels, one Bristol and another R.E.8 came flying into the vicinity. Lieutenants Palstra and Hamilton joined them in the attack, with Will flying the aeroplane and Hamilton working the machine gun.

"Swooped down on advancing Hun," wrote Will, "with engine full out and diving to 400 feet, petot showing 110 - 120 - 130 - 140 mph, and fired 400 rounds from Observers gun. One burst caught a party of 6 on the road east of Sequehart, killing five. Counter attack stopped just inside Sequehart. Huns holding east of village from which spot streams of "Buckingham"[61] were soon spurting towards me.

[Will's aeroplane] "Collected 'one' [burst of bullets] near this place, smashing the wireless reel and Klaxon horn. Carried on contact without Klaxon, coming low and swooping in circles over trenches at a good speed. Established the capture of a section of the Beaurevoir line and support line on a front of 2000 yards east of Joncourt."

Among the tanks and shells and bombs and machine guns, hundreds of thousands of horses were still playing a part in warfare.

"Watched an attack on Wiencourt and Riencourt with smoke shell barrage. Eight "Whippets" in reserve.[62] Saw some 1500 cavalry moving up towards the line from Bellicourt. Had a look at the ci-devant [former] impregnable Hindenburg Line from Bellicourt to Vendhuile…"

That famous Line had been, at last, well and truly broken.

---

61   Buckingham: Probably rhyming slang. Buckingham Palace = malice = machine-gun fire?

62   The Medium Mark A Whippet was a British tank of the First World War. It was intended to complement the slower British heavy tanks by using its relative mobility. Wikipedia.

Cutlack concludes the story of the breaking of the Hindenburg Line:

> "… the last obstacle, the Beaurevoir Line, was attacked on the morning of October 3rd by the 2nd Australian Division with the British. An R.E.8 was hit by a shell and two airmen from [No. 3] squadron were lost. The attack was rounded off next day by the capture of Montbrehain."

Advancing on the early morning of 5 October, the 6th Brigade A.I.F. succeeded in occupying the village of Montbrehain and in the process took 400 German prisoners. The action claimed 430 Australian casualties.

The Battle of Montbrehain was the last action involving Australian infantry on the Western Front in the First World War. The II American Corps relieved the Second Australian Division in the line on that very day. Together with the Division, the Australian Corps Headquarters also withdrew to the rest area on October 5th 1918.

The A.I.F. infantry had finally withdrawn from action.

The AFC, however, was still on active duty. From 5th October, No. 3 Squadron AFC stayed with the II American Corps, operating in the corps reconnaissance role.

The Beginning of the End

The tide of war continued to turn in the Allies' favour. The German army was plagued by exhaustion, illness, food shortages, desertions and drunkenness. Every day it was becoming weaker. Discipline and battle-readiness were waning.

The Allies were relentlessly advancing, and it was now clear that that they would be utterly victorious on the Western Front. Germany's General Ludendorff was at his headquarters when this realisation hit him so hard that he suffered a nervous collapse. He gathered sufficient strength to notify Field Marshal von Hindenburg that there was no alternative but to bring the war to a close with an armistice. The two high-ranking officers met with the Kaiser, who agreed with their proposal.

The first of the Central Powers to sign an armistice with the Allies was Bulgaria, on September 29, 1918. A new world order was dawning. The 600-year-old Hapsburg (Austro-Hungarian) Empire in central Europe now began to fragment. The new state of Yugoslavia announced itself, and Poland, once part of the Russian Empire, declared itself an independent state.

The war was not yet over, however.

No 3 Squadron AFC was still working closely with the American army. On 7 October Will was summoned to the 30th American Division Headquarters to discuss the "stunt of this Division towards Premont tomorrow". The following day was to be the culminating phase of the offensive on this front. The Americans hoped to break through to a depth of 6000 yards and let through cavalry, armoured cars and whippet tanks.

October 8 was Will's birthday but it's likely that nobody else knew about it.

"My birthday," he jotted in his diary. Such special days probably passed without celebration, when one was on active service. He was now 27 years old. This was the third birthday he'd had during his 33 months (so far) serving in the armed forces.

On that same day the British and Americans reached a line from Premont to Fresnoy-le-Grand, and next day took Bohain and Busigny.

From the runway at No 3 Squadron's aerodrome at Montigny Farm, Lieutenants Palstra and McDougall soared aloft on the morning of 9 October. They were off on a contact patrol with the 30th American Division on the line Busigny-Bohain.

Flying over northern France they established the fact that the Americans had advanced 5000 yards by 9 a.m. bringing the Front Line along and across a railway line running from west Busigny to west Bohain.

The roads were crawling with withdrawing blocks of German traffic, and there was no sign of any anti-aircraft batteries. The Germans were abandoning the whole country in front of the Selle River. As they retreated, they blew up roads and railways and set fire to villages.

From the air, Will and his observer witnessed scenes of destruction. The Germans had fired the Town Hall in Bohain, and it was enveloped in flames. The railway station had been reduced to ashes during the night, and another fire was starting to the east of the town. The two airmen also observed an explosion in the village of Bertry and a fire in St. Souplet.

As they continued their contact patrol flight, they noticed a couple of German battalions issuing in extended order from the village of Busigny, and guessed that the enemy's purpose was to mount a counter attack. Flying over the Germans at 2000 feet, Lieutenants Palstra and McDougall dropped a parachute flare to notify their own artillery. They also sent a wireless S.O.S. and fired red Very lights as a back-up.

Will then pushed forward the control column and his aeroplane descended to 500 feet.

Mc Dougall fired 700 rounds into the ranks of the advancing enemy, inflicting many casualties. The Allied barrage descended on the German battalions within five minutes of receiving the signals. The German counter attack was broken and the Americans, attacking in turn, took Busigny.

On their return home Lieutenants Palstra and McDougall looked down and witnessed the impressive sight of hundreds of cavalrymen galloping into action towards the Busigny-Bohain gap.

They also saw and took part in what Will considered to be "an effective bit of work … a unique instance of cooperation between infantry, tanks and aircraft." He spied troops advancing in artillery formation, and then noticed troops moving in open order ahead of them, apparently skirmishing through a series of little woods. Overhead, two Camels were flying. Every now and again the enemy would break out of one of those woods, and run across the open to the next. The Camels immediately dived on them, firing their machine guns.

This continued for about half an hour until it was clear that the American infantry advancing in the open from La Sabliere Wood were being held up by an enemy machine gun at Bertry Farm. A tank approached from the west, under cover of the woods, and sent three shells into the farm. The machine guns fell silent, enabling the infantry to advance. The enemy abandoned the place and several fell as three Camels and Will's R.E.8 dived on them, firing their machine guns. The aircraft dived in succession from the left flank, enfilading the advancing line, successfully stopping the advance.

A shortage of fuel made it necessary for Lieutenant Palstra's R.E.8 to leave, after that.

If you set aside the fact that this was bloody slaughter and mayhem on a grand scale, and accept—without judgement—the fact that Will was a man of his time, the purpose of whose job was to "kill or be killed", we can perhaps understand why he must have felt exhilarated by participating in a concerted four-aircraft machine-gun attack.

That afternoon No. 3 Squadron's Flights 'A' and 'B' bombed Le Cateau, and by the end of the day the cavalry were 2000 yards from Le Cateau.

On 10 October the American infantry was pushing forward past Busigny and Le Souplet, and roughly holding the line of the La Selle River. They freed numerous French civilians in Busigny and Vaux Andigny, where the villagers were flying white flags above their homes and waving to passing Allied aeroplanes.

Next day Will was up in the air on contact patrol with McDougall, between noon and 3 o'clock. They were peering over the side of their R.E.8 and probably using binoculars.

The Germans were attempting to build a line between the La Selle river and the railway embankment. Lieutenants Palstra and McDougall received isolated rifle fire from these trenches, which were evidently only lightly held. There was no machine-gun fire, and only one "Archie Battery" from east of St Souplet.

Soon afterwards they noticed smoke from a farm in St Souplet, half way between the Allied line and that of the Germans. On descending to have a look at this they witnessed the strange spectacle of an old French civilian piling manure on a heap in his yard, evidently cleaning stables, seemingly careless of the fact that his place formed a No Man's Land between two hostile lines.

Other civilians were trooping out of St Souplet wheeling barrows and prams containing their few belongings and pushing west through the American Lines.

Truth is often stranger than fiction. In the midst of battle, appalling scenes occurred but also incongruous events which might be bizarre or comic, such as Will's sighting of that French farmer calmly going about his chores while war blazed all around. Similarly, it is recorded that during a fifteen-minute halt in an attack on 23 August 1918, one Australian infantryman merrily played a piano found in a deserted hut.[63]

The dawn of hope

A copy of the Continental Daily Mail newspaper arrived at No 3 Squadron's current base, Montigny Farm 'Drome' on 13th October. It contained news of the acceptance by the Central Powers of the American President Wilson's Peace and Armistice Conditions. For the first time there seemed to be a genuine glimmer of hope on the horizon. Could peace really be within reach at last? What a stir this news must have caused among the airmen of No. 3 Squadron!

"Will this mean the end of the War?" Will wondered in his diary—
> "Germany has stored up some deadly hate for herself, and justice and public opinion in Allied Countries especially France will demand stern punishment."

The Battle of the Selle took place between October 17th and 26th, 1918. The Germans were now occupying a new position, immediately to the east of the Selle River. They were in a state of extreme fatigue, and the Allies knew it.

CW Bean wrote,
> "The German Army wanted time to rest and reorganise, and could almost certainly have obtained it had General Ludendorff been willing to withdraw... but [he] desired a stand to be made in order to influence the Armistice negotiations by a show of resistance..."[64]

---

63   P. 740 Vol. VI, Bean

64   Bean, Vol. VI

The German commander Erich Ludendorff was not happy with the peace terms that were being discussed with the Americans. He felt that they were humiliating to Germany.

Bean again:

> "Field Marshal Douglas Haig decided to strike while the Germans were near exhaustion. He ordered a series of operations designed to get British troops in strength across the Selle river."

Aided by no 3 Squadron, AFC, American General Henry Rawlinson's army struck again on October 17th. Lieutenants Palstra and Hamilton flew low over the landscape, peering down at the countryside. Presently they spotted a counter attack of approximately two German battalions deploying from Bazuel and advancing in open order towards a sunken road. Hamilton dropped a parachute flare through the clouds. They backed up this signal with a wireless S.O.S. and also dropped a message on a British 18 pounder gun battery. Having alerted the artillery, they flew over the German battalions, strafing them with Vickers and Lewis fire.

Rawlinson's army drove the Germans across the Selle River and took le Cateau.

Said CW Bean:

> "The Germans now retreated to the Sambre-Oise Canal, where it became evident they would try again to stand. Haig was determined to go on hitting them and German histories show beyond question that he was right."

The German Army was swiftly being hunted out of France.

In all, between 27 September and 18 October 1918, Lieutenant Palstra carried out ten Contact Patrols, and directed artillery fire on three counter-attacks.

On 19 October British troops from IX and XII Corps arrived to relieve the Americans. The RFC would provide aerial support for the British units, which meant that No 3 Squadron was left, in the words of its commander Major David Blake, "without a corps to work with".

The squadron was ordered to stand by in reserve, and to supply artillery patrols for the British troops whenever they were needed. For Will, being in reserve meant more free time, at least in the foreseeable future. The Australian airmen decided to take the opportunity to take a self-guided tour around the local area. It was a surreal time to be in France, as Will's diary indicates:

"19.10.18. Hamilton, Ellis and I went lorry hopping to Le Cateau today. Found the town much knocked about. Machine gun being fired from the tops of some of the houses and 18 pounders barking, showing that the war must still be pretty close to this place. Roamed through an abandoned Feldlazaret, formerly a huge weaving mill, and souveniered a Pickelhaube[65], bugle, belt, photos, proclamations etc. Still a few civilians in the town. Was present whilst R.E. [the Royal Engineers] removed huge quantities of explosives from the Church belfry. Hun motor transport with the drivers dead, standing in front of the Hotel de Ville, had iron tyres, another proof of shortage of rubber. In the Lazaret [a hospital] bandages and nightdresses were nearly all made of paper."

From Will's Diary:

"20.10.18 Latest news, our troops in the North have reached the Dutch frontier. Captures of prisoners and material are huge. Aeroplanes were the

---

65   The Pickelhaube, or Pickelhelm, was a spiked helmet worn in the nineteenth and twentieth centuries by German military, firefighters, and police.

first to enter Ostend, the Pilots landing and ascertaining that the town was evacuated.

"21.10.18 Hamilton and I went "lorry hopping" [hitch-hiking] to Bellenglise and the St. Quentin Canal this morning. Examined the remains of a twin-engined A.E.G. Bomber evidently brought down by a Comet. Also a Junker armour plated two-seater.

"22.10.18 Weather dud—no flying. Walked to Brancourt Le Grand with Hamilton. There is an underground labyrinth in this place, dug by the Huns as a Casualty Clearing station. The entrance comes out under the main road near the Church, and the Tommies [British troops] who occupied it said the place was 400 yards deep."

The next day, 23 October, the weather must have cleared, because Lieutenants Palstra and Hamilton were flying in their R.E.8 again. Around 12.25 they were flying at 2000 feet over Catillon when enemy machine guns opened up on them. One bullet smashed through the tail of the plane and another pierced the main spar of the right bottom wing. This last one spattered to pieces, spraying Lieutenants Palstra and Hamilton with particles of lead and fabric—the flimsy fabric that formed the plane's skin. Noting that the bullets had emanated from six machine gun emplacements in houses along road east of Catillon, they dropped six 20 lb Cooper bombs on those emplacements.

The airmen must have developed a taste for exploring the territory once held by the enemy, because on 26 October Will—

"Made a day of it with Hamilton and Barret. Lorry hopped to the St

Quentin Canal, and explored this, including its tunnel under Bellicourt and the ramifications of the Hindenburg Line. The whole defensive system is extremely strong, tunnels leading to machine gun emplacements forming a leading feature. There are deep and spacious dugouts capable of holding thousands of men with galleries and passages feeding points along the whole front. The Canal tunnel had been filled with barges providing accommodation for troops. Here again numerous tunnels lead to various parts of the fighting line. The ends of the tunnel have a thick cement wall loopholed for machine guns."

Clearly, men become hardened to daily carnage. On the afternoon of 27 October, Will cheerfully "took Captain Dobson, M.C., A.L.O. to the Squadron, for a joyride."

They flew over Bohain, le Cateau, Cambrai and St Quentin. He wrote,

"Cambrai seems much knocked about. An area of several acres in the centre of the town is entirely razed to the ground. Cathedrals in both St. Quentin and Cambrai are badly damaged."

28 October was especially interesting for Will because it was on this morning that he and Lieutenant Hamilton went (probably on foot or hitch-hiking) to the spot where they had brought down the enemy Albatross on 27 September.

"Found wreck of machine," he recorded—

"Our machine gun fire had caught him in the engine and probably killed the pilot. Longerons and engine bearers were also cut by bullets. The engine, an 8-cylinder Mercedes, had fallen out of machine before she struck the ground, and machine had then sideslipped into ground crumpling up left wings. All instruments had been salved [salvaged] by enemy. Plane marked all over with letters B.F.W. and No. 2929. Made a report of this to Wing on return home."

Seeing the wrecked aircraft must have been, for Will, akin to a hunter viewing a stag he had bagged. It was the same for all military airmen, a source of motivation and pride, and army headquarters knew this.

> "In the morning of 29 October official word came through from "Wing" "confirming our aerial fight on 27th Sept and ordering that we be officially credited as having brought down EA on that date."

As an afterthought Will added, "Dropped 3 bombs on Toaillon Wood."

The fighting men had no way of knowing how close they were to the end of the Great War. They had to keep risking their lives on a day-to-day basis, while far away the politicians sat in conference discussing the terms of peace. The troops in combat on land and sea and in the air could not know whether an agreement would be reached soon, or later, or indeed, ever.

A pandemic

Late in 1918, armistices were being signed all over Europe. Something else of global importance was also unfolding: the beginnings of a pandemic.

Cutlack writes,

> "Faced with mutiny, the defeat of her allies, and the exhaustion of her civilian population, Germany had no option but to open peace negotiations. Moreover, both servicemen and civilians became afflicted with the so-called 'Spanish influenza', which swept across the globe, becoming the greatest killer of the century so far. Thus, to all the demeaning horrors of the trenches was added fever."

Will was fully acquainted with the spread of this deadly global pandemic, of course. He may have already fallen victim to the "flu" in November 1917, and recovered from it. If it was indeed the Spanish Flu he was suffering from, then he was among the earliest patients. Officially, the first cases did not begin to appear until January 1918.

Between February 1918 and April 1920, "the pandemic infected 500 million people—about a third of the world's population at the time—in four successive waves. The death toll is estimated to have been somewhere between 17 million and 50 million, and possibly as high as 100 million, making it one of the deadliest pandemics in human history."[66]

The enemy retreats

On 4 November in France, No. 3 Squadron was preparing to accompany the British 25th Division in an attack on the French town of Landrecies, which had been in German hands since they captured it in August 1914.

At 4am that morning Will was lying awake in bed listening to the roaring sound of the Farmans and Handley Pages passing overhead on their way to the Line. The noise of their engines enabled the Allied tanks to crawl up to the jumping-off line unnoticed.

He was up, dressed, breakfasted and on the Drome by 5.30, but it was a cold morning and because of this the Bristol Fighters would not start for a long while. At 6 a.m. a thick fog blew in on a southerly breeze, effectually obscuring everything and making landing and taking off impossible. Fifteen R.E.8s had already left the ground to do smoke screening.

These machines had to remain in the air until 7.30 when the fog cleared.

Nothing could have been more useful to the launching of the attack than this sudden and providential fog right on zero hour.

"It almost seems an act of judgement on the Hun," wrote Will. "Screened by this efficient cover the infantry were able to overcome the serious obstacle

---

66 Spreeuwenberg P, Kroneman M, Paget J (December 2018). "Reassessing the Global Mortality Burden of the 1918 Influenza Pandemic". Am. J. Epidemiol. Oxford University Press. 187 (12): 2561–67. doi:10.1093/aje/kwy191. PMC 7314216. PMID 30202996] and [Rosenwald MS (7 April 2020). "History's deadliest pandemics, from ancient Rome to modern America". Washington Post. Archived from the original on 7 April 2020. Retrieved 11 April 2020.

of the Canal de la Sambre a l'Oise without much difficulty."

He took the air at 8.30 a.m. to do a reconnaissance of the enemy back areas, and stayed over the Line for two hours. During that time he witnessed an aerial combat from a distance. "Two planes were brought down, one in flames—a ghastly sight when you are in the air."

CW Bean writes about that evening:

> "… aeroplanes reported that all roads ahead were crowded with retiring Germans. Next day the Australian artillery was withdrawn. Only the cavalry could keep up with the Germans in their retreat. So effectively had the enemy demolished railway and road junctions and bridges that food and munitions could barely be supplied to the pursuing troops, and delayed-action mines constantly wrecked other key points in areas now behind the British front.
>
> "In an interchange of notes, following Prince Max's appeal for an armistice, President Woodrow Wilson had insisted that he could not treat with the German Government unless it withdrew from the invaded territories…" [67]

Will wrote in his diary on the 5th November:

> "Austria signs Peace. Notice outside A.L.O.'s[68] office sums up the situation nicely:
>
> BULGARIA) TURKEY) NAPOO AUSTRIA)
>
> NOW FINISH—THE HUN!

On the morning of 7 November, the officers of No 3 Squadron received a wireless message to the effect that a German commission had left Berlin the day before, bound for the Western front, to discuss terms of an Armistice with the Allies. This delegation,

---

67   Bean, Vol. VI

68   A.L.O. is probably "Air Liaison Officer"

consisting of two admirals and two generals passed through La Cappell on the way to Paris that very afternoon at 3 p.m.

These were encouraging tidings!

Further reports confirmed that the Americans had captured Sedan and Messieres, advancing a remarkable thirteen miles in two days. As the month progressed, huge changes swept through Germany.

CW Bean reported,

" …on November 9th some of the airmen flying over French or Belgian towns behind the German lines could not find an enemy to shoot at. The streets were thronged with people; German soldiers were among them. A revolution, though almost a bloodless one, had happened in Germany. The Social Democrats had insisted that the Kaiser and Crown Prince must go. The German Republic was proclaimed from the steps of the Reichstag. At the front, German soldiers mingled with the villagers, believing—so says an Australian prisoner of war—that they would now be treated as brothers by the enemies who had been exhorting them to fling off their militarist leaders."[69]

That evening Will wrote to his parents in Australia. He had sent gifts of Australian Flying Corps brooches to his sisters Hetty and Blanche. In his mother's last letter, she had confirmed that they had received the gifts and were very pleased with them. Another family member must have wanted one too!

"O" Flight R.A.F.

OAS France

---

69   Bean, Vol. VI

9/11/18

My darling Mother & Dad,

The past week has brought your letter dated 17/9/18, and also a parcel—my birthday parcel I take it. Speaking of the parcel first—this was ideal, and quite the best of the many delightful ones that have come my way. It contained:- 1 pair of socks, tin of butter, potted meat, packet of sugar, cocoa (containing sugar and milk), chewing gum, toffee, and chocolate.

Every one of these items were just the thing, and came in very handy, especially as we are living more or less on our rations at present owing to growing distance from railhead and Base.

The letter—the only one by this mail so far—was welcome as always, and assured me that all at home were well, and doing well. I have written to England for an A.F.C. brooch Mum, and shall send this on as soon as I get it. Pleased to hear the girls liked theirs.

You will wonder at the address in the righthand corner of this letter, I am attached temporarily to the Royal Air Force. I can't give you many particulars, as the unit is a bit of a speciality, but sufficient to say that it is quite a small affair.

Having started writing this letter, Will set it aside for a few days. His life had become very busy again—too busy for keeping up with correspondence.

On 10 November "O" Flight became part of an independent force of the RAF, and moved to Flaumont, east of Avesnes. It was on the occasion of ferrying his aeroplane to Flaubert that Will was involved in his first accident.

"On landing I run into a sunken road which crosses the new Drome, and in a twinkling reduce my beautiful machine—a Rolls Royce Bristol Fighter—to matchwood. Got out of the wreck without as much as a scratch. This is my first crash."

Suddenly, almost unexpectedly, on 11 November 1918, at 11 o'clock an amazing thing happened…

Cutlack reported, quoting Will's words,

> "Meanwhile, down south at No.3 Squadron's forward landing ground at Flaumont, pilots were preparing to take off when news arrived that fighting would stop at 11.00am. Bill Palstra recorded how the airmen 'reluctantly' switched off their engines and climbed down. 'Strafing a retreating army is good sport to the man in the air,' he explained, 'though probably far from agreeable to the Hun plodding back to Hunland.'[70]
>
> "At 11.00am, Palstra and some of the other airmen were sitting around, debating whether the news [of the armistice] was true or not, when a great racket sprang up all around the countryside. Cheers and the sound of bagpipes filled the air, along with hundreds of Very lights. 'We stood still and listened,' wrote Palstra in his diary, 'and the realization dawned on us that this was the end of the war'…"[71]

It was true.

The Great War was indeed over.

A wonderful thing has happened

Historian Anthony Livesey explained that, "Prince Max of Baden, the newly appointed German chancellor, accepted President Wilson's terms, a republic was proclaimed and the

---

[70] This quote does not appear in the Palstra diaries held by the family. It's clear that war had changed Will, as it must change everyone. Look back to early 1916, when a mild-mannered city clerk was worried about whether to join the Medical Corps so that he would not have to break the sixth commandment, then look at the close of 1918 and see a fearless pilot ruthlessly manoeuvring his aeroplane and machine gun to mow down the enemy…

[71] Cutlack, "Fire in the Sky" p.325

Kaiser fled to sanctuary in Holland. A German delegation agreed to Allied terms—virtually unconditional surrender—in Foch's railway carriage at Compiegne on 11 November and hostilities ceased at 11:00 on that day."[72]

"The 1st and 4th Australian Divisions were then arriving in the region about le Cateau," wrote CW Bean. "Neither there nor at the front was there any general demonstration—the sound of guns ceased; the gates of the future silently opened. Wonder, hope, grief, too deep and uncertain for speech, revolved for days in almost every man's mind..."[73]

11 November 1918 was 'Armistice Day'. Hostilities ceased and the First World War officially ended. Bells rang out, and the music of bagpipes, and the cheering of human voices.

From Will's diary:

"11.11.18 At 9 a.m. this morning the following wire was received from 4th Army.

'An Armistice has been signed between the Allied Powers and Germany, and will take effect from 11.00 (French time) today. Units will not advance beyond the Line held at that hour. Necessary precautions will be taken.

'There will be no intercourse with the enemy. AAA.'

"A town crier with a bell was soon spreading the news amongst the civilian population. It appeared to me that they thought it too wonderfully good to be true. Here as everywhere they tell the same tale of harshness, extortion and cruelty on the part of the Hun. Towards the end the Huns themselves had little or nothing to eat, and the lot of prisoners, especially

---

72   "The Viking Atlas of World War I", Anthony Livesey, Viking, 1994. 66 Bean, Vol. VI

73   Bean, Vol. VI

English, was pitiable. Before leaving, the Hun looted everything he could carry away with him.

"Walking towards Avesnes I suddenly heard a mighty cheering and the sound of pipes[74]. Looking at my watch I saw it was 11 a.m. They were Dorsets[75] and H.L.I. [Highland Light Infantry].

"Coming along the road were a family of refugees returning to their homes. The woman carrying a little girl, and the man pushing a pram containing their few belongings. The bells of Avesnes commenced to ring, the pipes were still playing and the troops cheering.

"They stopped to listen—I told them the news—"*La guerre est finis. Nous avons vaincu. C'est la victoire.*"

He replied, "*Ah, monsieur, nous sommes bien heureux—Vive l'Angleterre.*" To which I replied, "*Vive la France.*"[76]

"These people to me seemed to typify the spirit of France—tired, worn, having suffered much, but caring only that the victory had been won and "the day of glory had arrived."

"Left for Grand Fayt[77] at 4 p.m. Arrived 1 a.m. 12.11.18."

Will had free time on his hands—an unusual experience for him. He took this opportunity to finish writing that letter to his parents.

---

74   The rallying tunes played by bagpipers had an important function for British troops during the First World War.

75   Possibly the Dorsetshire Regiment.

76   "The War is over. We have won. It is victory." "Ah, sir, we are very happy. Long live England." "Long live France."

77   Grand Fayt: a commune in the Nord department in northern France.

19/11/18
No 3 Squadron A.F.C.
Premont FRANCE

Ten days have elapsed since I commenced to write this letter, and a wonderful thing has happened—it is hard to realise it—hostilities have ceased.

I look at the moon and say to myself, I wonder when the first Hun bomber will come over tonight. But all is silent, no guns, no searchlights, no gasmasks, no tin hats. It's wonderful, it is a new world. Let us hope it will be a better one.

One splendid feature is that the Censorship has been abolished or relaxed, and it is allowed to give the names of places, units etc. So here goes. I am, and have been for the past 6 weeks at a little place called Premont between Bellicourt and Le Cateau. In fact during the past 3 months my Squadron has been following up the Hun in an almost continuous battle from Peronne to Avesnes, and I have taken part in every one of these battles—up to the Hindenburg Line—the great smashing of the H L [Hindenberg Line] on Nov. 29th—the smashing of the Beaurevoir Line on my birthday Oct 8th. —the battle of the La Selle River—and finally the battle of the Canal de La Sambre a' l'Oise on Nov 5th.

Now that it is all over you won't be alarmed when I say that I had a pretty strenuous time.

My machine has been riddled with bullets on more than one occasion. But I have come through without a scratch, although I nearly killed myself the day before the Armistice was declared, by running my machine into a sunken road at 40mph. My beautiful Rolls Royce engined Bristol Fighter was smashed to smithereens, but I crawled out of the wreck feeling not even shaken.

To continue my rambling remarks—5 pilots were picked from the Squadron to form a special 4th Army Flight, known as "O" Flight. We were given the best machine yet made—the Bristol Fighter. Our work was scouting, and reconnaissance 8 to 10 miles over Hunland. My speciality was taking oblique photos at low altitudes far over Hunland. For instance I photographed the back of the Hun Sambre Canal Line at 800 ft. running the gauntlet of machine gun & rifle fire. For this work I was "mentioned" twice in Wing Orders in one week.

Then "O" Flight was transferred to the famous Independent Force R.A.F., so that I can claim to have done service with that.

How did the 11th find me? The situation was most strange. We had moved to a new Drome 5 km E of Avesnes the day before. Here we found the infantry in billets behind us—the Drome in a N.M.L. [No Man's Land] of about 5000 yds depth, and only groups of Cavalry between us and the Hun.

The Civilian population were delighted to see us, especially as we shared our rations with them. They had had a very unhappy time under the Hun. On the morning of the 11th at 9am a wire came through. "An Armistice with the enemy has been signed and will take effect from 11.00. Troops will not advance beyond the Line held at that hour. All precautions will be taken. Aeroplanes will not cross the Line."

Guns fired salvos of blank, troops & civilians cheered—and—the war as far as the fighting went, finished...

Everything had changed. It was time to lay down arms, time to say goodbye to war and return to civilian life. But this could not happen overnight.

On 13 November 1918 "O" Flight was disbanded. Lieutenant Palstra had only just returned to No 3 A.F.C. at Premont. He had resourcefully hitched a ride on a tender (a trailing vehicle coupled to a steam locomotive to carry fuel and water), arriving at 9 o'clock that morning.

Straight away he learned that he had been awarded four days' leave in Paris "as a reward for good work", with his comrade Charles Matheson.[78]

---

[78] It was after he returned from that sojourn that he wrote the above letter—dated 19th November—to his parents.

Leave in Paris

The two flying-officers travelled to Amiens by air and from there by train to Paris, arriving at 8.30 p.m. on the same day. They stayed at Hotel Prins Albert in the Rue Hyacynth near the Place Vendome.

> "Had four rollicking good days seeing Paris sights & joining in the crowd's celebration of the Victory," wrote Will. "... that wonderful city where everyone reflects the happiness felt by the nation—heroic France, now that her day of glory has come at last. It is a wonderful finish, and France can hardly realise her good fortune. Millions of flags are waving from the houses. 'C'est la victoire!!' after 4 1/2 years of suffering and bitter fighting. Can you imagine it all?"

The Great War was over. They had survived. They were young and free, and soldiers were especially popular with the young women of Paris. One can only imagine what an ecstatic, uninhibited four-day celebration that was! One Australian soldier's experience was published in the newspapers:

```
The Journal (Adelaide, SA: 1912—1923)

Sat 18 Jan 1919 Page 7

IN PARIS.

ARMISTICE DAY CELEBRATIONS.

[By Lce.-Cpl. N. V. Wallace, A Company, 48th Battalion.]

It was my good fortune to be on leave in Paris on that day
of days, November 11, when the German delegates signed the
armistice which marked their final downfall. Perhaps, too,
that signature will mark the birth of a Greater Germany,
founded on those democratic principles which time and events
have proved to be the only means by which a nation may hope
to maintain its honour and prestige in the counsel halls of
mankind.

Leaving my hotel about 10 o'clock, I made my way along
the boulevards to the British Leave Club in the Place de
la Republique. Something about the city crowds seemed to
foreshadow the great news which was soon to send them all
half-crazy, for the 72 hours allotted to the German delegates
was almost at an end. Groups of allied soldiers sat at
tables in the streets toasting the arms of their countries
and wondering if the proud militarists of Germany would be
content to accept the humiliating Allied terms, and surrender
once and for all their hopes of ever attaining a place in the
sun by force of arms. Not that any of them cared much for the
general opinion expressed or unexpressed, was everywhere the
same, "If they don't like our terms, they can leave them.
We're quite willing to fight on till they do like them."

In the club the excitement was intense, but it wasn't long
before we were informed of the great news.
```

Strangely enough, we didn't go mad straight away. It was more than the lads could realize. All that one could really understand was that Germany had acceded to terms, and that fact alone was too much for us to take in all at once.

Did it mean that we would not rejoin our units to be hustled up the line; were we never again to hear the shrieking sigh of the approaching shell, the spiteful zip of the sniper's bullet, or the rustling whirr of the falling bomb? Could it be that the long nights of watching were over, that the muddy trenches were really a thing of the past? Had Verey (sic) lights, the parachute flares, and artillery signals flashed out on the blackness of no-man's land for the last time, and were we never again to line the tapes at dawn, amid the deafening drumfire of barrage and counter-barrage preceding the attack?

Surely these things could not be?

There in the hall and on the stairs we discussed the situation, Tommy, Maori, Jock, and Digger, Canuck, Guardsman, Enzed, and Springbok men gathered from the ends of the earth, assembled in happy unison at the home of the Empire's sons in Paris, beneath the majesty of that symbol of liberty, the Union Jack, the defence of its honour had drawn them one and all from farm and office, from hall and cottage, to risk their lives in a foreign land.

—The Procession.—

Presently one of the ladies of the club announced that a procession would take place in the afternoon, starting at 2 p.m. Every one, of course, had to be decorated, so out we went. The drapery shops nearby were raided, much to the amusement of the petite mamselles inside, who took charge of operations, and soon had our hats and caps adorned with tricolour bows and streamers.

Returning to the club we soon had it stripped of all its flags, and by 1.30 p.m. were lined up outside awaiting the arrival of the Royal Horse Guards' Band, which was to lead us on our triumphal march.

The procession was headed by a small group representative of Great Britain, and all the colonies each one bearing the flag of his native country, and with us were little V.A.D.[79] nurses and girl guides from the club. Behind us and a little to the rear, two tall guardsmen carried a huge Union Jack — then came the band, and then a cheering flag-waving throng of British, French, and American soldiers, with dozens of pretty little Parisiennes scattered among them, cheering and singing.

Our starting point was at the foot of the Statue of Liberty, in the Place de la Republique, surely symbolical enough, but made more so by the fact that the Union Jack was held just over the spot where one of Big Bertha's messengers of hate had erupted its burden of spite and chagrin upon the undisturbed Parisians just two or three months before.

Turning into the Boulevard St. Martin we made our way by various routes to the British Embassy. All along the way the excitement was terrific. Every one seemed to be singing. The band played "La Marsellaise" time and again to the accompaniment of thousands of voices. Bunting had sprung up from nowhere, every one had a flag or a heap of red, white, and blue ribbon.

Shopgirls waved kisses from the windows, perhaps wishing that they were down with their sisters, who were not content with the waving part of the business. Almost every soldier had both arms fully occupied, while some one else carried his flag for him.

At the Embassy Lord Derby realizing the futility of words just waved a flag and cheered, joining heartily in the singing

---

79   Voluntary Aid Detachments

of the National songs of the Allies.

Passing onwards down the Champs d'Elysees, we entered the Place de la Concorde, where hundreds of trophies of war are collected. Here, at the foot of the statue to Alsace-Lorraine, we halted.

Once more the band struck up the National songs. Once more the crowd yelled and cheered. Standard bearers of all nations mounted the steps of the statue and stood to attention with the purple and white flag of the Yugo-Slav Republic held high in their midst by representatives of the Slav Legion attached to the French Army.

Passing onwards we came to the Place Vendome. Here in the crush the vanguard was separated from the main body, and so we pushed our way back to the Place de la Republique, through the cheering excited crowd.

—For France.—

After dinner we went out once more to see the fun. In the glory of their once more illuminated city the Parisians gave themselves up in a spirit of wild abandon to their emotions. Looking down along the great boulevard, now bright as day in the glare of the great arc lamps, one could see nothing but a swaying, laughing, cheering, flagwaving crowd, at one in their delight in the downfall of the dirty Boche ("La Sale Boche"[80]) as they call him. Greybeards in the cafes clinked their glasses toasting "La Revanche,"[81] thinking of those other days when the conquering hordes had defiled these places with their presence.

But to the younger generation revenge was not the uppermost thought. They were warm-blooded Gauls, happy, passionate,

---

80   "The Dirty Boche"

81   The payback

and above all, human, bubbling over with love and laughter, seemingly forgetful of the sufferings and horrors they had borne so nobly these past years. And yet not forgetful, for under all their gaiety lay the memories of slaughter at Verdun, of doubt and fear on the Marne. But what of that! Was it not for La France? The tricolour cockade enlivened the dresses of black[82] — the black was but personal, the colours were national. And what spirits, what life.

Close your eyes a minute and picture the dazzling boulevard. Here a crowd of happy midinettes[83] prance up and down, arm in arm with their boys in khaki and horizon blue. Now they collide head on with another such procession — and catching hands in the medley, form a surging circle around the centre. Round and round they go singing and cheering till tired by their own exhilaration, the little girls fall into the arms of the nearest soldiers, whose kisses restore them once more, and on they go again.

What a people for kissing they are. On occasions such as these every little midinette considers herself altogether out of it if she is not kissed by every allied soldier who passes within embracing distance. The Frenchman quite understand the situation — they are of the same warm temperament themselves, but the average Britisher, not forgetting the bashful Digger, has not been used to such an orgy of endearment. Still in this, as in other critical periods, of his experience abroad, he rises to the occasion with a zeal that is more than commendable, acquitting himself as nobly in the groves of Venus as he has done on the field of Mars[84].

All night these scenes went on. "No sleep till dawn, when

---

82 Black for mourning

83 Midinette: a seamstress or assistant in a Parisian fashion house.

84 'The groves of Venus': love and romance, 'the fields of Mars': warfare.

youth and pleasure meet," and even at dawn the crowd was great, so I presume the stopouts were reinforced by the early risers.

The estaminets and cafes were open all night, and though always filled to overflowing with the brave and the fair, not once did I see a Parisian really drunk, or zig-zag, as they most happily call it. This was certainly not through abstinence, for liquors of all kinds flowed like water, so one is brought to the conclusion that they take to it as naturally as we in Australia take to tea, if not more so.

—"Cest La Paix!"—

In a few days they will finish their laughter and singing, and will settle down to build anew their half-shattered country as they did in those tragic years of the early seven-ties, sacrificing anything and everything for their beloved mother "La Belle France." They need no other inspirations, their country's needs are theirs, her wish, their law, and so long as she calls upon them they will face all suffering and sacrifice with a merry laugh, and a ready jest.

Good luck to them.

"Vive la France et les Francaises."

Armistice Day celebrations in Paris, 1918. Wikimedia Commons
wiki Category: Paris_in_World_War_I - First found on Dec 17, 2014

Charles Bean summed it up: "The end of the war had come almost as suddenly as its beginning. On August 21st [1918] the Allies were still planning for the next summer's campaign. In less than three months, fighting had ended and the British oversea dominions were faced with the urgent problem of getting their forces home—'Repatriation'.[85]

It was time to think about going home.

---

85   Bean Vol. VI

Armistice Day celebrations in Paris 1918
americanphotoarchive.photoshelter.com image/I0000YVOtT3QJMQ0
First found on Aug 13, 2009

For the armed forces, however, the process of repatriating thousands of men, sending entire battalions back across the sea in ships, required a huge amount of organisation. It would take months.

Lieutenant Palstra knew it might be a long time before he set foot on Australian soil and was reunited with his beloved family.

On 17 November he (probably accompanied by his friend Matheson) returned from Paris to No 3 Squadron's billets at Premont. Here he spent two days in bed with a bad cold.

Charles Palstra

While Will was recuperating in bed, in walked his brother Charles!

Will was delighted, surprised and relieved.

> "Get a visit from Charles," he wrote happily in his diary, "and have a rattling good yarn with the old boy. It is wonderful that we have both come safely through this world holocaust."

Knowing that his parents were hungry for news of Charles, as soon as possible after the visit he cabled them a telegram; "Both well Going Bonn".

He followed up the telegram with a letter:

> "I had Chas here both yesterday and today, [18th and 19th] and we yarned for hours. There is none of the swelled head about him, and a nicer fellow would be difficult to find. The last couple of years have matured him wonderfully. Conversation never flags when he is about, and he has a fund of humour which will make him welcome everywhere. In short quite the kind of brother to be proud of. We hit it A1!
>
> "He is looking well, although he is feeling the strain a bit I think. Thank goodness it is all over. What a merciful providence has kept us both through so much death and destruction. We look forward to our jour de gloire, not far distant now I hope, when we shall be reunited again. Thank God for his goodness."

No 3 Squadron moved to Charleroi on 27th November, aided by ground transport. Will had more time to write letters, now, and to explore the devastated countryside for miles around.

And then he was granted leave.

"1.12.18 Awakened at 5.30 a.m. and told my Paris leave has come through. Leave by car at 7 a.m. and catch the train for Amiens at Bohain at 2 p.m.

"Travel in a cattle truck all night with some Tommies and two families of French refugees returning from Belgium to their homes in France. As it was cold the Tommies built a wood fire in the centre of the truck. It gave much smoke but the warmth was agreeable. We shared our rations with the refugees who will certainly have pleasant memories of their treatment by 'Les Anglais'. One little girl of about 10 soon made friends with me, and we chatted for hours about the Hun, her Daddy—a prisoner of war, and Australia. Towards 1 a.m. she commenced to nod drowsily so I took her in my arms and with her pretty little head on my shoulder she was soon contentedly asleep."

Will went on leave in Paris twice—first from 11 to 23 November and then from 8 to 28 December 1918, after which he returned to work "On command at Engine Workshops".

The Australian War Memorial's website explains, "Despite the war being over, and Australian troops not constituting part of the Allied occupying force in Germany, it was to be a long time before many Australians would return home. The day after the armistice, Private A. Golding wrote: 'They told us we would be another 12 months in France.'

"Repatriation to Australia was organised by Lieutenant General Sir John Monash, on a first come, first go basis. While awaiting transport, some men took advantage of the opportunity to travel around France and Britain- one of the incentives for enlisting in the first place…

"During this period of limbo, the AIF instituted a range of education and lecture programs to train personnel in peacetime occupation skills. In a letter to his mother in late 1918, Sapper W.M. Telford wrote: 'I am enclosing a prospectus of our AIF education scheme. I think it is a splendid idea and intend to take full advantage of it.'"[86]

---

86 AWM 1918: Australians in France—Home at last—the Australians return

Letter from Will's mother Jacoba:

'Carrigmore', Middlesex Road, Surrey Hills.

27.12.18

My dear Will,

I just heard that on Monday next a mail is going out, so I must sit down and write you even if it will be only a little note. Days are very much occupied this time of the year, all the Xmas festivities where I have to be present are all crowded in a couple of weeks.

Well my dear boy, we have had a very enjoyable time, the first time in four years that one dared to be happy and show it too. Just fancy no war and fighting going on and the look out, that you boys may come home sometime next year, it is really glorious. All hopes are fixed for next year—a united family on Xmas day.

… Everybody was home on Sunday and we had a very nice time together.

I have never seen Dad so jolly in all my life, on these children's parties in the [Salvation Army children's] homes, he gave himself entirely for the amusement of them. Even the Commissioner, old Scot that he is, collapsed, when the four Colonels present gave a rod drill[87] in imitation of an item of the girls.

… When I had gone through your most interesting letter, I could not help saying, what a fighter this boy of mine has become, and the worst of it is, that he warms up his old Dad too, after he has read your letter, he looks as

---

87   "The senior girls, with polished brass rods, gave a fine exhibition of rod drill, and one wondered how they were able to twist their wrists with such swiftness." From an article entitled "SALVATION ARMY", describing "A fine entertainment given in the Memorial Hall, Healesville." Healesville and Yarra Glen Guardian (Vic. : 1900 - 1942) Sat 22 Jun 1935 Page 3.

though he could go and fight the Hun too. A good job things have come to an end, I really don't know what the next would be.

We are going early to Mentone[88] this year, next week by this time the house will be packed up and the next day (Saturday) we depart early. I am looking out for a real good time…

The neighbours have offered to look after the chickens, and I take a family of 24 chicks with us, and coming back I shall get a dozen ducklings from a farm there, our own came suddenly to grief. So you see I have got it all planned out, there will be plenty of fowls and eggs—when the boys come home!

We got your parcels with this mail too, my word he (Frank) was pleased with this bomb inkwell, he'll tell you all about it himself, it went straight to the bank to be admired by the friends. John got a watch for Xmas box, it nearly took his breath away. The joy I have got out of it is, that at six in the morning he is already in my bedroom, to verify his watch with Dad's, of course it must not lose a minute.

December 31.

…The next mail will be the first after the Armistice, we eagerly look out what news it will bring. Thank the Lord for good news from Charlie, he seems quite recovered.

We spent the day yesterday at Riddell[89], temperature 96 degrees [35.5C] in the shade, it did not seem to dampen the ambition of the gents for cricket.

---

88   Mentone is a seaside suburb of Melbourne where the Salvation Army maintained a holiday resort for officers.

89   Riddell's Creek, a rural town in the state of Victoria.

They looked like perspiring beetroots, dear Dad included. We all had a great time. Tomorrow we shall be at Bayswater and that will finish up the festivities and then Mentone. I just feel I can do with a couple of weeks rest.

God bless and keep you my dear boy, With love from your everloving

Mother.

Christmas in France

Will spent Christmas in France with No 3 Squadron. He continued his duties "on command" at the Australian Flying Corps' engine repair workshops in that country from 7 to the 17 January, then at the British 4th Army Electrical School from 5 to 14 February, 1919.

In Versailles, not far away from where Lieutenant Palstra was working, the Peace Conference commenced on 13th January. At the same time, civil war was raging in Russia.

Principally, the Bolshevik Red Army fought against the White Army. Many foreign armies warred against the Red Army, notably the Allied Forces, and many volunteer foreigners fought on both sides.82

Since the middle of 1918 the deadly influenza pandemic had continued to spread across the world. The 'Spanish Flu' was killing people throughout the northern hemisphere and even in New Zealand. Quarantine measures were being enforced in Australia.

Back in Australia Will's family—particularly his parents—existed in a continuous ecstasy of happiness. The Great War was over, and their two soldier sons had not only lived through the carnage, they had emerged covered with glory. And they would soon be coming home.

Will kept in touch by cable, to assure them that all was well.

In Will's father's letter of 13 January 1919, he writes about the family's joyful anticipation of the boys' safe return home. His happiness is slightly clouded by the knowledge that his own six-year stint in Australia is almost at an end. The Salvation Army's policy was to move officers to a new location, in a new country, when six years had elapsed, and families had no say in where they were to be posted. Just as the Palstras were about to be reunited, they were in danger of being torn from each other once again.

PART III
1919: Repatriation

Will wrote to his parents on 31 January 1919. At that time he could see no other option than to depart for Australia on the SS Kaiser-I-Hind[90] in May, with the other members of the Australian Flying Corps. So many thousands of troops were being repatriated at this time that Australians, like the other men of the Empire's dominions, had to wait for months to get passage on a ship. Wounded soldiers had first preference. For the rest, it would be a long and frustrating wait of many weeks until they could finally go home. Meanwhile, the airmen occupied themselves as best they could.

Will, however, was impatient. He could not endure the thought of waiting for months to rejoin his family in Australia. Voyaging with the AFC meant getting a free ticket, but he yearned to reach home sooner, so he and his comrade Lieutenant Knight stumped up

---

90   The SS Kaiser I Hind was an ocean liner that before the onset of the First World War served the route to India. When war broke out, she was requisitioned as a troop transport ship. Her name is Hindi for 'Empress of India' [Imperial War Museums]

their own money and bought tickets for the SS Kildonan Castle. This three-masted, twin-funnelled British hospital ship was due to leave Devonport, England, on 21 March, with the job of repatriating wounded troops to Australia. Will decided not to inform his parents of his early arrival—he would surprise them!

Mail travelled slowly in 1919. Cable telegraph could not always be relied upon, and the events described in letters often took place well before those letters reached their intended readers. When family in friends in Melbourne heard of Will's imminent homecoming—in May, as they thought—they could barely contain their excitement.

Salvationists did not merely worship together on Sunday mornings; their social lives revolved around the other members of the Corps. The Palstras' news percolated through the entire tightly-knit Salvation Army community of Melbourne. When Will had departed from Australia with the 39th Battalion in May 1916, the shy ex-clerk, his mettle untested in active service, had been barely known to most of them beyond a nod of recognition.

All that had now changed.

Every Melbourne Salvationist—and almost every Salvationist in the country—had been hearing, for months, about the achievements of the son of the Chief Secretary to the Salvation Army in Australia. Will's leading of the 39th Battalion at the Battle of Messines, his being presented with the Military Cross medal by the King of England himself at Buckingham Palace, his feats of daring in the Australian Flying Corps—his brave exploits had become almost legendary. Lieutenant Palstra, MC, AFC was a hero, and they all longed to have him back in their midst, and to claim him as their own. The month of May seemed far away, and it was hard to wait patiently.

Certainly the Holdaways, that well-known Salvation Army family from New Zealand, would have heard all about Will's exploits. Widowed Mrs Brigadier Holdaway and her children, including her daughter May, would be as keen as anyone to follow the news concerning returning soldiers.

Meanwhile Lieutenants Palstra and Knight embarked on the steamship Kildonan Castle on 21st March, and headed across the Indian Ocean, bound for Australia.[91] Steamship passenger lists were regularly published in the newspapers, so their imminent arrival in Australia would not long remain secret.

Letter from Wiebe to his son Will:

Melbourne 17.4.1919

My dear old Boy,

We are all in a flutter of excitement, possibly this note may give some trace of it—however, let me just give you the facts.

On Monday last I was phoned up by Blanche [Will's sister], who is working in the City, and told that an acquaintance had just been to see her with the startling information that your name was amongst the number listed as returning by the Kildonan Castle. Frankly I did not believe it was true for your latest letter to hand, dated 31.1.19, impressed us that you felt then, it was likely you might be detained for quite a little while longer. Besides you not only promised us in that letter you would cable us, in the event of sailing and as this was so much in harmony with your uniform practice, throughout the

---

91   Back in London, any remaining members of the A.I.F. and AFC who had not yet departed for Australia took part in several famous parades through the city, beginning with "Anzac Day" on 25th April 1919. In Australia and New Zealand, ever since, returned soldiers, sailors and airmen have marched through the streets of their various state capital cities each year on Anzac Day.

whole period of your absence, I felt pretty well sure, the news was too good to be true, seeing no cable had arrived. (I am now concluding it has somehow miscarried.)

However I phoned up the Red Cross folk from whom the message emanated, they stated it was quite correct and furthermore that the vessel was due at Fremantle on April 24th and at Melbourne, barring quarantine restrictions, on May 2nd. Confirming this I have now received the official intimation from the Defence Dept. Hence our excitement! It's just splendid to feel you are almost now, at the time of writing, in Australian waters and that this will reach you upon arrival at an Australian port.

Ten thousand welcomes—let me say this straightaway, leaving it to the actual arrival in Melbourne, to say it again then only ever so much more perfectly. The news of your homecoming has created quite a flutter here at Headquarters, amongst the folk who know you and who, I may say, have the utmost respect for you.

If I followed my feelings literally, I'd be organising a kind of glorification in which all our [sic] Melbourne could take part. As it is we shall arrange to suitably, warmly, enthusiastically and lovingly receive, with profound gratitude to God for having preserved you to us and with a thrill of pride and satisfaction that our man has pulled things off so well. Hip, hip!!

I can hardly make any suggestion as to plans etc. for the immediate future; probably we shall confine our attention to the welcome and after that other matters can be talked over and decided upon.

You can't have got one of my latest letters sent to London in which I stated that I heard from an Hon. Secretary of the Repatriation Committee that the Repatriation authorities, upon production of proof that prior to enlisting it was his intention to study, give a full course at the University free of charge plus a weekly sustenation [sic] allowance of £2 while at the University. Put in your claim, even prior to disembarking for it can easily be proved you intended to study and that the wherewithal was the only drawback.

We're all in ripping form, your early return has greatly bucked us. Trust the trip was agreeable. May He who has watched over you hitherto continue His presence with you.

Much, much love,

Yours ever,

Dad.

Homecoming

On 7 May 1919, Will returned home to Melbourne at last.

The Melbourne newspaper "The Argus" ran articles asking that, "Owners of motor cars who are willing to assist are requested to notify the secretary of the Royal Automobile Club, and to be in attendance with the cars at the pier... at the expected time of a troop-ship's arrival."

This preference for motor cars over trains stemmed from the need to care for the wounded soldiers, many of whom would have been seriously disabled.

```
The Argus (Melbourne, Vic.: 1848-1957)

Thursday 8 May 1919, Page 7

TROOPS DISEMBARK.

Men from Kildonan Castle.

Owing to the satisfactory response of motor-car owners no
difficulty was experienced in transporting to the city 510
troops who disembarked from the transport Kildonan Castle at
```

```
Port Melbourne yesterday morning. The men left the ship at 8
o'clock and during the preliminaries before they boarded the
motor cars at 9 o'clock were welcomed by the State commandant
(Brigadier-General C.H. Brand) in a breezy speech, which
contained sound advice as well as glowing appreciation.. .
```

Soldiers disembarking at Port Melbourne in 1919. AWM H13025

Visualise the exuberant welcome that awaited Lieutenant William Palstra! Crowds congregated on Station Pier, filled with emotion as they waited impatiently to meet the returning troops. Did they cheer, to hide their distress as Red Cross nurses ferried young soldiers down the gangway in wheelchairs, while other men hobbled forth on crutches, their heads or arms or legs bandaged.[92]

---

92 Eric Bogle poignantly describes the return of a First World War hospital ship to Australia in his famous song "And the Band Played Waltzing Matilda".

Wounded Australian soldiers disembarking in Australia. AWM 100329

No doubt Will's entire family was waiting among those crowds, probably accompanied by a large contingent of Salvation Army folk who were keen to set eyes on the returning hero. Was young May Holdaway among this contingent? Certainly she would have known all about his achievements; "The news of your homecoming has created quite a flutter here at Headquarters…".

Will was indeed a hero of the Great War, decked with medals to prove it.[93] In addition to the Military Cross, he had been awarded, (like his fellow veterans), the British War Medal and the Victory medal. Imagine him at Station Pier striding down the gangway of the SS Kildonan Castle in his lieutenant's uniform with a smile on his face, his kitbag slung over his shoulder, his comrade by his side, bands playing, crowds cheering, car horns honking. He had been tested in the pits of hell, and had passed the test with flying colours. He had discovered qualities in himself that he had never suspected – courage, resourcefulness, determination, a new-found confidence. And he would soon be in the arms of his beloved family! The future glowed before him, bright and exciting.

And this, for now, is where we leave him.[94]

The 39th Battalion

What of Will's old battalion, the 39th?

They had spent October of 1918 in the French village of Hocquincourt in Picardie, France, while the armistice was being negotiated. The grateful villagers treated them with kindness.

The battalion's commander, Lieutenant Colonel A. T. Paterson wrote,

> "Time passed quickly until November 11. When the momentous news was received that the armistice had been signed there was a singular lack of the enthusiasm which might have been expected from the 'diggers'. Their feeling was rather one of immense relief from the tremendous strain which had told so much upon all.

---

93 To sum up Will's wartime flying career: he had specialised in low flying, including ground strafing and oblique photography. He had had ten successful contacts, spotted three enemy counter-attacks, and had brought down one enemy aircraft (officially credited). He was one of a select few seconded for duty with "O" Flight in the Royal Air Force, the "Special Bristol Fighter Flight" involved in long distance low oblique photography and reconnaissance.

94 Will's appointment as a member of Australia's armed forces was officially terminated on 21st June 1919.

"It meant more to these men than could be realized in a moment. The gloomy shadow of war which had been cast over them for nearly three years had been lifted as if by magic. The days of suffering, horror and death were over for most of them. Soon—for the first time for years—they began to speculate about the future; life seemed worthwhile again.

"The great objective had been reached at last – peace for the world and the prospect of future happiness."

In February 1919, with France in the grip of an icy winter, the demobilization of the Third Division began.

"At last," wrote Paterson, "the 39th ended its days of active service and left France for home. The men were sad and glad in leaving France—sad for the comrades left behind forever; glad for the family re-unions to follow.

"Many an unmarked spot in France must be forever Australia. The youth and flower of Australia's manhood died valiantly fighting for their country and, by their sacrifices, laid the foundation of a Nation.

'LEST WE FORGET'"[95]

The 39th Battalion was disbanded in March 1919.

The story of the 39th does not end here, however. The battalion would be raised again during the Second World War and its story came to be "one of the most unusual and proudest in the annals of Australian military history." [96]

---

95   Paterson "The History of the Thirty-ninth Battalion AIF"

96   Australian Infantry Battalion (1941/43) Association Inc.

A bouquet in memory of the 39th Battalion AIF, laid in tribute at Melbourne's Shrine of Remembrance on Anzac Day 2006. The memory of the First 39th is honoured to this day due to the efforts of Mr Tim Fitzgerald.

The end of the brotherhoods

The war's end brought mixed emotions to the men who had fought shoulder to shoulder for so long as a band of brothers. It was a momentous shift in the courses of their lives. Everything changed for the men when they came home to civilian life. It was, in some ways, a bitter-sweet change. Here was the peace they had fought for, the families they had missed. But gone was the camaraderie, the sense of purpose, the feeling that they were part of a mighty, energetic, terrible machine.

The author of the official history of the 49th Battalion AIF (whose members hailed from Tasmania) gives us an idea of what repatriation felt like for the troops returning to Australia in 1919:

'The first draft left [France] on the 17th February 1919, and it was only then that we realised that this brotherhood of men existed no longer as a battalion of infantry. For quite two days before this draft departed there was a feeling of irresponsibility about all of us. We drank in fellowship together, pledged ourselves to meet again in Tasmania and … for once felt sorry that the war was over. Those of us who remained stood in the rain and watched the draft move off. Farewells were shouted, mostly facetious, with reference to future meetings in favourite Tasmanian hostelries. But as the column moved beyond us we stood watching them in silence as they plodded away from us through the mud and rain, till they passed out of sight …"

In memory of The Australian Imperial Force (AIF)

In 1941 C. E. W. Bean[97] wrote:

"The Old Force passed down the road to history. The dust of its march settled. The sound of its arms died. Upon a hundred battlefields the broken trees stretched their lean arms over sixty thousand of its graves.

"... When the A.I.F. first sailed, it left there a nation that did not know itself.

Even the 1st Australian Division entered its first battle not knowing what manner of men Australians were. The people of the six states which formed the Commonwealth were much divided. Many an Australian had no confidence in the capacity of his people for any big enterprise.

"...It is in disaster that human character is most clearly exhibited, and though she had known fire, drought and flood, Australia had never seen the

---

97   Bean, Vol. VI, Chapter XXII "The Old Force Passes"

one trial that, despite civilised progress, all humanity still recognises—the test of a great war.

"And then during four years in which nearly the whole world was so tested, the people in Australia looked on from afar at three hundred thousand of their own nation struggling amongst millions from the strongest and most progressive peoples of Europe and America. They saw their own men—those who had dwelt in the same street or been daily travellers in the same railway trains—flash across the world's consciousness like a shooting star. In the first straight rush up the Anzac hills in the dark, in the easy figures first seen on the ridges against the dawn sky, in the working parties stacking stores on the shelled beach without the turning of a head, in the stretcher-bearers walking, pipes in mouth, down a bullet-swept slope to a comrade's call, unconsciously setting a tradition that may work for centuries…

"Australians watched the name of their country rise high in the esteem of the world's oldest and greatest nations. Every Australian bears that name proudly abroad today and by the daily doings, great and small, which these pages have narrated, the Australian nation came to know itself.

"Twenty-three years ago the arms were handed in. The rifles were locked in the rack. The horses were sold. The guns were sheeted and parked in storage for other gunners. The familiar faded-green uniform disappeared from the streets.

"But the Australian Imperial Force is not dead. That famous army of generous men marches still down the long lane of its country's history, with bands playing and rifles slung, with packs on shoulders, white dust on boots and bayonet scabbards and entrenching tools flapping on countless thighs—as the French countryfolk and the fellaheen of Egypt knew it.

"What these men did nothing can alter now. The good and the bad, the greatness and smallness of their story will stand. whatever of glory it contains nothing can lessen. It rises, as it will always rise, above the mists of ages, a monument to great- hearted men; and, for their nation, a possession for ever."

A 2016 article on the Australian War Memorial website is entitled, "1918: Australians in France—Home at last—the Australians return."

"The Aftermath of the War.

"It is not unusual to read of men and women who returned home after the war "not being able to settle down" or "having a go at everything" because they weren't sure what to do with their lives. Many were restless for months or years after their experience in the war.

"Thousands of Australian men were killed in France in 1918. The memories of their deaths, however, were to remain forever with those who had witnessed them. Some service personnel, upon returning after the war, were so traumatised by their experiences that they could not talk about them. Hundreds of thousands of men returned to Australia with permanent injuries- reminders of all they had experienced, and physical reflections of how the war had changed them.

"There was also a sense of bitterness that people who had not served in the war would never understand exactly what it was like for those men and women who had.

"However, there was a strong sense of national pride in what the Australian troops had accomplished during the war, and the significance of their contribution was felt by soldier and civilian alike. Cities and towns began to build war memorials to Australian service personnel, with 60 being completed even before 1918. Today, there are approximately 2,000 war memorials all over the country, large and small, inscribed with the names of the men from each community, school or business who were killed. These memorials take many forms, from a single soldier statue to a memorial gate or arch, usually situated in prominent and public places."

AIF Captain Ivor Williams' last entry in his war diary, on 5 February 1919:

"Thus my diary ends after relating some of the most enjoyable, interesting, educating and saddest times in my life. One has a clear conscience though, that he, at least, tried to do a little for those at home we love better than all things on this earth. After nearly four years I now close this diary and enter civilian life a very much wiser man, thanks to the army and to "Kaiser Bill and his cobbers".

GOODBYE."

The Number of the Fallen

What were the total casualties of the Great War?

Encyclopedia Britannica[98] tells us that world-wide, there were around 40 million military and civilian casualties during the First World War, with 20 million dead and 21 million wounded.

According to the minimum estimate of the principal belligerents, the Central Powers lost three million, five hundred thousand soldiers on the battlefields of the Great War. The Allies (also known as the Triple Entente) lost five million, one hundred thousand men. On average, this was more than five thousand, six hundred soldiers killed on each day of the war.

The total number of deaths included from 9 to 11 million military personnel. The civilian death toll was about 6 to 13 million. At least 2 million died from diseases and 6 million went missing, presumed dead.

The legacy of the war—the physical and mental suffering, the consequences of shell-shock, mental breakdown, the loss of limbs and health, the devastating effects of grief—was to continue for many, many years.

---

98 "World War I—Killed, wounded, and missing | Britannica". Britannica.com. Retrieved 5 December 2021

In all, 61,522 Australians lost their lives in the First World War. As well, an estimated total of 664 Australian officers and 17,260 men were wounded. [99]

The enormity of the sacrifice of this young and idealistic generation can only begin to be understood when you visit some of the hundreds of Commonwealth War Graves Commission cemeteries that are scattered throughout northern France and Belgium.

Have you forgotten yet?...

For the world's events have rumbled on since those gagged days,

Like traffic checked a while at the crossing of city ways:

And the haunted gap in your mind has filled with thoughts that flow

Like clouds in the lit heavens of life; and you're a man reprieved to go,   5

Taking your peaceful share of Time, with joy to spare.

But the past is just the same, and War's a bloody game....

Have you forgotten yet?...

Look down, and swear by the slain of the War that you'll never forget.

~ Aftermath (Siegfried Sassoon)

THE END

of

BLOOD AND FIRE

VALIANT HEART BOOK 3

---

99   Source: Australian War Memorial.

If you have enjoyed this book, please review it on Amazon or Goodreads.

Goodreads: https://www.goodreads.com/

Amazon USA: https://www.amazon.com/

Amazon UK: https://www.amazon.co.uk/

Amazon Australia: https://www.amazon.com.au/

For freebies, news and promo codes from Leaves of Gold Press, visit our website.

https://www.leavesofgoldpress.com

Visit the Airship of Dreams channel on YouTube @AirshipofDreams and the Leaves of Gold Press channel, @LeavesofGoldPress

AIRSHIP OF DREAMS

The Doomed Flight of the Titanic of the Skies

VALIANT HEART 1

"Airship of Dreams" is a true story. It stands alone and can be read by itself, although it is also Book #1 of the VALIANT HEART trilogy. The book tells William Palstra's extraordinary life story; a life that ended in 1930 when His Majesty's airship R101 exploded catastrophically, changing the world forever.

An Air Force pilot and decorated hero, Palstra returns to Australia in 1919, at the end of the First World War. We follow his marriage and family, his role in the expansion of Melbourne University, and his rise through the ranks of the newly-formed Royal Australian Airforce (RAAF).

The decade of the 1920s was the Golden Age of Airships and zeppelins. The stuff of dreams, these enormous, cigar-shaped aircraft glided slowly and majestically across the skies, like fantastic creatures from legend.

The British Empire's R101 was the world's biggest airship at that time. She was fitted out so luxuriously that she has been called The Titanic of the Skies. And like the Titanic, her maiden voyage was doomed.

"Airship of Dreams" tells of this fatal flight, and the repercussions of the tragedy that rippled through time and continues to exert its influence to this very day.

Valiant Heart Trilogy

Book 1: Airship of Dreams
Book 2: The Call to Arms
Book 3: Blood and Fire

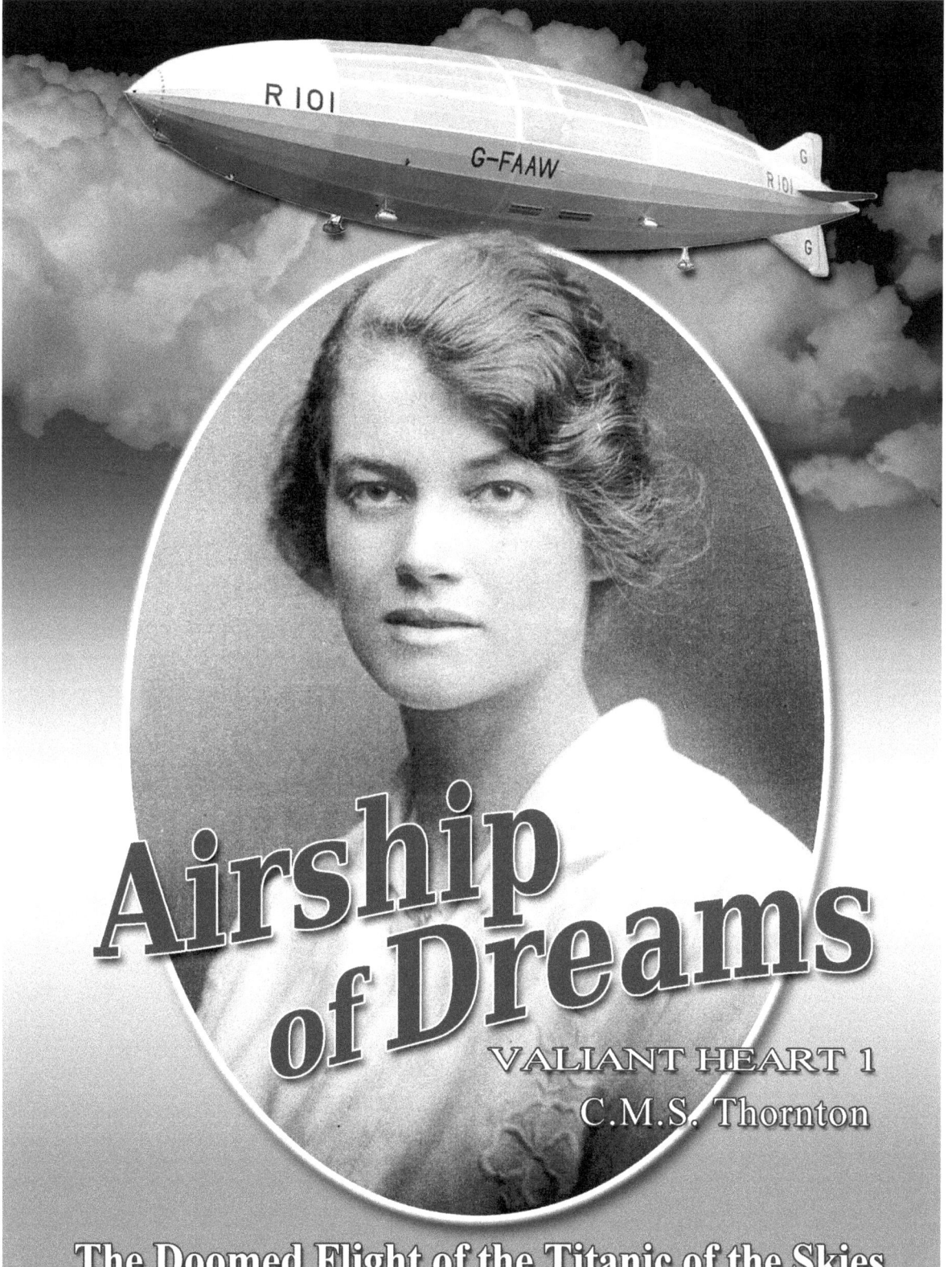

THE CALL TO ARMS

The Office Clerk Who Dared the Great Adventure

VALIANT HEART 2

This is the biography of First World War hero William Palstra between 1914 and 1917. An office clerk in London sails across the sea in a steam-powered ship and becomes an office clerk in Melbourne, Australia. The Great War commences and his younger brother enlists in the Australian Imperial Force (A.I.F.), becoming an Anzac. Will Palstra enlists in 1916, trains at Ballarat in Victoria, and voyages back to Britain with the 39th Infantry Battalion. They complete their training at Stonehenge on Salisbury Plain and cross the English Channel to begin active service on the infamous Western Front.

"The Call to Arms" is Book #2 of the VALIANT HEART trilogy following Palstra's well-documented life story as he comes of age, maturing from a mild-mannered office clerk to a commissioned officer in the Australian Army.

Valiant Heart Trilogy

Book 1: Airship of Dreams

Book 2: The Call to Arms

Book 3: Blood and Fire

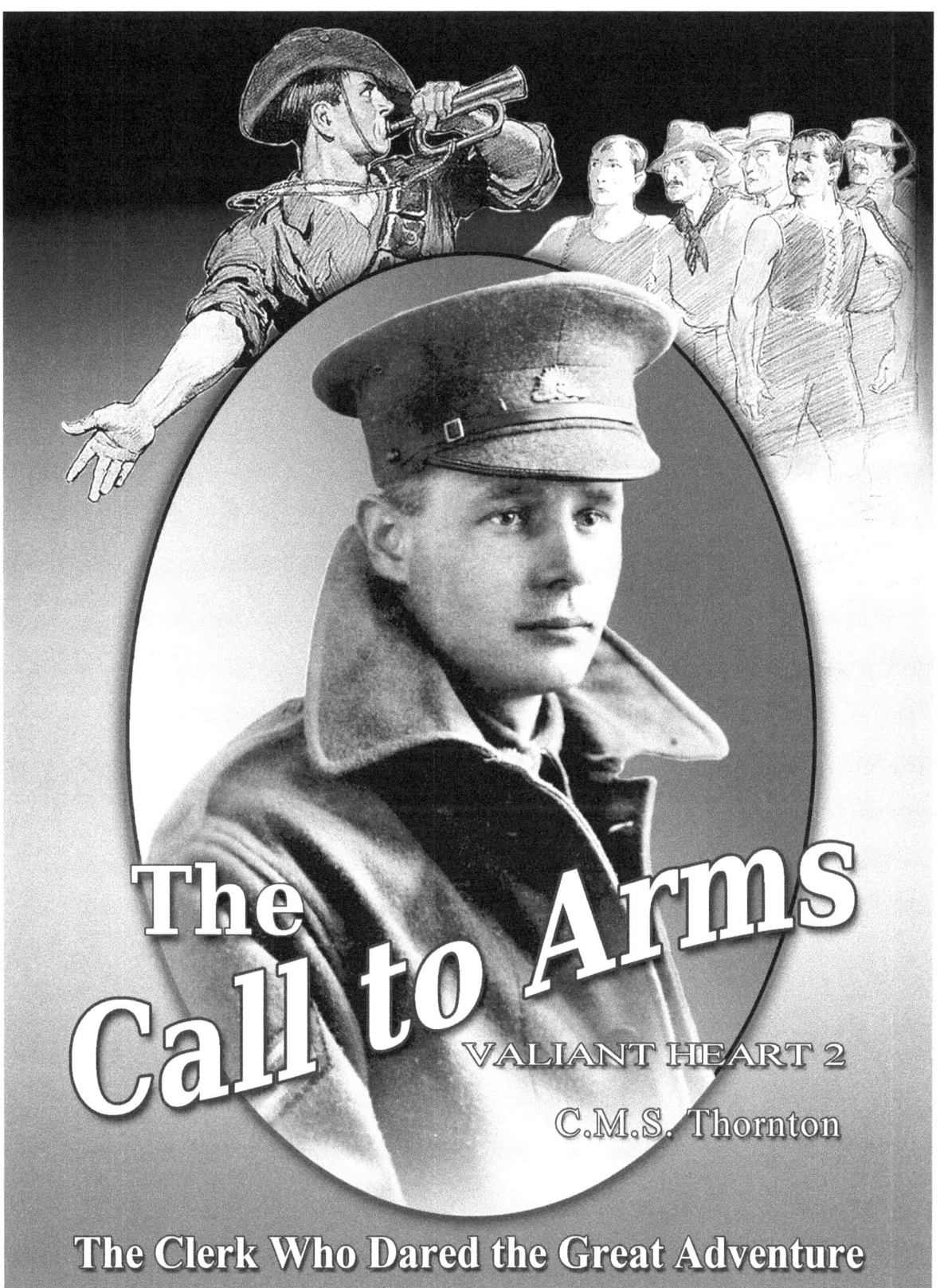

The Call to Arms

VALIANT HEART 2

C.M.S. Thornton

The Clerk Who Dared the Great Adventure

www.ingramcontent.com/pod-product-compliance
Lightning Source LLC
Chambersburg PA
CBHW061211230426
43665CB00032B/2977